DOERS OF THE WORD

AMERICAN ACADEMY OF RELIGION
DISSERTATION SERIES

edited by
H. Ganse Little, Jr.

Number 18

DOERS OF THE WORD

Toward a Foundational Theology
Based on the Thought of Michael Polanyi
by
John V. Apczynski

SCHOLARS PRESS
Missoula, Montana

DOERS OF THE WORD

Toward a Foundational Theology
Based on the Thought of Michael Polanyi
by
John V. Apczynski

Published by
SCHOLARS PRESS
for
The American Academy of Religion

Distributed By

SCHOLARS PRESS
University of Montana
Missoula, Montana 59812

DOERS OF THE WORD

Toward a Foundational Theology
Based on the Thought of Michael Polanyi
by
John V. Apczynski
St. Bonaventure University
St. Bonaventure, New York

Ph.D., 1972   Advisor:
McGill University   Dr. Joseph McLelland

Library of Congress Cataloging in Publication Data
Apczynski, John V.
    Doers of the word.

    (American Academy of Religion dissertation
series ; no. 18)
    Originally presented as the author's thesis,
McGill University, 1972.
    Bibliography: p.
    1. Knowledge, Theory of (Religion) 2. Polanyi,
Michael, 1891-   I. Title. II. Series:
American Academy of Religion. Dissertation series -
American Academy of Religion ; no. 18.
BL51.A62 1977   191   76-51640
ISBN 0-89130-128-3

Printed the United States of America
1   2   3   4   5
Printing Department
University of Montana
Missoula, Montana 59812

PREFACE

My aim in this study has been to explore the problem of the meaning of religious belief and the grounds for upholding its validity. The method I have chosen to investigate this fundamental issue consists in an analysis of human cognitional activity based on the epistemology of Michael Polanyi. Consequently this study implies that Polanyi's theory of knowledge provides a valuable approach to understanding the problem of human knowledge in general and that this in turn can serve as a basis for understanding religious claims as well. Accordingly Polanyi's position is presented in terms of its intrinsic logic in order to lead into the religious question, and the argument which attempts to substantiate this is a gradually unfolding one.

After a description of the problem to be explored, Polanyi's critique of the dominant ideal of impersonal objectivity and its cultural consequences, which he terms moral inversion, is detailed. Its purpose is to provide the background for Polanyi's insistence on the personal factor in all forms of knowledge. Once this is recognized, however, a coherent account of this personal involvement which sustains the objectivity of knowledge must be provided. This account begins in the third chapter by examining our cognitional activity through the categories developed by Polanyi. Here his proposal that all explicit knowledge is dependent on a tacit base is introduced. Substantially this consists in the claim that all knowledge is a comprehending of subsidiarily known particulars into an explicitly known whole. Structurally the activity of knowing forms a continuum ranging from basic inarticulate skills to the highest levels of theoretical knowledge. By "dwelling in" the particulars, be they bodily impulses, linguistic patterns, or cultural world views, we expand our mental existence and open

v

ourselves to increasingly greater degrees of comprehension. An initial examination of the problem of validating our acts of comprehension and our explicit affirmations shows that such acts are not subjective if they are made responsibly, with what Polanyi calls universal intent. But when the panorama of the historical flow of intellectual and cultural assumptions is considered, Polanyi's analysis indicates that the validation of our knowledge may be sustained only because our claims to universal intent entail a bearing on reality. How can this exigency of personal affirmation be taken into account?

This stage of the problem is explored in the fourth chapter where the logic of Polanyi's position finally leads us to outline his comprehensive vision. Structurally tacit knowing always has a bearing on reality, orienting all human activity toward understanding some aspect of reality. In order to substantiate this claim for the structure of tacit knowing, an excursus is taken so that the notion of "reality" is situated in the proper context of Polanyi's thought. This includes his understanding of levels of reality and man's place in the evolutionary process. From this vantage point the objective basis for the continual development of human thought is shown to be grounded in the "experience of ultimacy." This kind of experience, which is uncovered through the cognitional analysis, is a condition of which we are tacitly aware. It qualifies all our acts of knowing and is the tacit base enabling us to uphold our explicit claims.

The argument as it has been unfolded thus far provides the framework for moving to the question of religious belief. Its meaning can now be understood as an attempt at "breaking out" toward the source of the experience of ultimacy. Because this is the source of our knowledge and not an aspect of it, it can never be comprehended in the technical sense. Hence the need for "revelation," symbolic language, religious traditions, and faith. Furthermore, theology as a discipline can be understood to mediate intelligently the meaning of this experience within the culture at large both to adherents of the faith and to those outside the community of faith.

This very brief synopsis attempts to highlight the course of the argument. The fundamental implication is that man is a being who is shaped by the activity of his knowing. In its basic sense this implies a faithfulness to reality, whereby one's doing is informed through the experience of ultimacy toward ever greater comprehension of the real. To the extent that a person does this successfully, to that extent does he grow. In its religious sense this faithfulness to reality implies that man's knowing, and thus his being, is transformed by becoming a "doer of the Word," because in this case the growth is a call toward the Mystery of Infinite Reality.

ACKNOWLEDGMENTS

The completion of this work has been facilitated by various degrees of assistance from many quarters. I would like to single out three of them.

First of all, I am indebted to Loyola College of Montreal for a teaching assistantship which enabled me to pursue my studies at McGill. Even more beneficial than this, though, has been the opportunity it provided for me to grow in theological understanding through discussion with my former colleagues there.

The members of the Faculty of Religious Studies at McGill University have also contributed substantially to my development. In particular I owe much to my advisor, Dr. Joseph McLelland. His advice and constructive comments, beginning with the formulation of an idea all the way through to its final expression in this work, have proved to be invaluable.

Finally, I wish to thank my wife, whose presence and patience have been an unquenchable source of inspiration.

CONTENTS

CHAPTER I

THE SCOPE AND LIMITS OF THE PROBLEM

One of the most urgent problems facing the religious believer today is belief itself. Unlike the problems of even a
generation ago when the most pressing concern may have been to
modernize literalistic or fundamentalist interpretations of
traditional doctrines, the contemporary predicament goes deeper
still. In an era dominated by a scientific conception of reality, relativized by a historical consciousness, and closed in
by secular preoccupations, religious belief appears to be so
many meaningless words and outmoded gestures. The contemporary
challenge to religious belief is thus radical: the very foundations of belief are at stake. This fundamental problem is
the object of this inquiry.

The scope of this study, then, consists in the attempt to
provide an explanation which can establish the meaning and validity of religious belief and theological understanding. The
investigation is limited, however, to the exposition of a method for achieving this aim. The issue, in other words, is not
any particular religious doctrine or the "objective truth" of
any specific religious tradition. References will indeed be
made to religious beliefs and theological positions, and furthermore these will be drawn predominantly from the Christian
tradition. Whenever such instances are presented for consideration, they are to be taken as illustrative, rather than constitutive, of the problem. Such a limitation of the analysis
to a general exposition of the foundations of religious belief
hopefully may permit a potential extension of its results beyond the limits of our specific illustrations by theologians
from other religious traditions.

Posing the question at this radical level, however, raises

1

a complementary question: On what basis are we to base our
investigation? The import of this difficulty can be clarified
by contrasting it with a typical methodological inquiry. In
the natural sciences, such as physics, both the object and the
methods for understanding the object are already given and pre-
sumed to be valid. Here a methodology theoretically expresses
a logically consistent account of the procedures of the science. Clearly our concern cannot be termed methodological in
this typical sense. Since the meaning and validity of religious belief are in question, the problem is one of foundational theology.

This means, first of all, that we envisage the problem as
a philosophical one. In order to ground theological understanding, we must reflect beyond typical explicit formulations
of methodology to a more fundamental level which accounts for
the activity of the human mind in upholding a methodology.
Yet, because of the problematic, it is not simply philosophical, for it has a theological preoccupation and undoubted theological implications. Our proposal, then, is to analyze the
cognitional activity of man, including how he knows and what
he knows, and to explore this in such a way that the meaning
and validity of religious belief might be established. Finally, upon this basis a schematic outline of the method appropriate to theological understanding may be indicated. The
problem should thus be understood in this reciprocal way, where
the validity of religious belief is assessed by means of a
foundational analysis and the foundational inquiry is guided
ultimately by the attempt to clarify a theological problem.

Since the proposed foundational theology will be developed
by means of a reflective analysis on human knowing, the precise
way in which this is undertaken is of considerable importance.
To carry out this task, we have adopted and adapted the theory
of knowledge articulated by Michael Polanyi.

A few words may be appropriate at this juncture to indicate briefly some of the reasons for using Polanyi's analysis
of human cognitional structure and his incipient ontology. As
is well known, there has been and, to some extent, there still
is a confusion as to the relationship of the physical sciences
to the life sciences, an ambiguity concerning the role of the

social sciences, and an uneasy feeling flowing through the human sciences. Much of this is due to the acceptance, implicit or explicit, of physical science with its seemingly clear and distinct kind of knowledge as the paradigm case of knowledge and measuring other kinds of "knowledge" by this criterion. The revolution within physics earlier this century had precipitated a vigorous re-examination of these assumptions. The meticulous and arduous development of logical and linguistic thought represents one major aspect of this re-examination. Another is to be found in the emphasis on the human as a distinct sphere of knowledge apart from objective, scientific knowledge proposed by some existentialist philosophers. These two "poles" have dominated speculative thought for most of this century. What seems to be emerging now is a convergence. Existential-phenomenology is becoming more involved with the question of language; linguistic thought is beginning to recognize the existential and ontological meanings of language.

In the midst of these movements stands Michael Polanyi, whose career as a scientist and whose peculiar concerns in analyzing the truth which the scientist seeks and the functions which the scientist performs have enabled him to analyze the situation outside of current vested interests and to propose a theory of knowledge that we believe has grappled with the issues raised by both movements. In stating this we are not, of course, implying that Polanyi is the *only* one who has attempted this. Rather, it indicates simply that we have found the proposals of Polanyi stimulating and would like to explore their implications for theological understanding.

The program Michael Polanyi has developed he calls "personal knowledge." It has as its central thesis "the fact that *we can know more than we can tell*"[1] or, more technically, that knowledge can never be totally focal, but must rely on a subsidiary base.[2] This subsidiary base, which has later been developed and expanded by Polanyi as the tacit dimension, resides in the person, indeed could be called the person insofar as he has assimilated his culture's tools—be they skills, words, logics, or theoretical disciplines—and by dwelling in them is enabled to relate *to* reality. Knowing is a process of life, and in man it takes that particular form of process we call history. Knowing is thus an activity that we do, which we perform, by opening ourselves to being and its ever expanding horizon and at the same time and through the same process by becoming ourselves.

This brief description encapsulates Polanyi's position. In the course of our exposition, we shall attempt to explain what this means and particularly what it implies for theology. There will be, accordingly, no attempt to detail the development in Polanyi's thought. His early, more exploratory works will be discussed only insofar as they contribute to the clarification of his mature position. This appears in publications during the mid-1950's, especially in *Personal Knowledge*, and in his later works.

Polanyi himself hints at many points that his theory of personal knowledge has applications beyond those he explicitly formulates, including theology.[3] As an aid in developing Polanyi's thought in this direction, we shall rely on works by theologians that have some affinity here. These will come primarily from the Catholic theological tradition and are generally termed "transcendental Thomists." The development of Polanyi's thought will be aided by these theologians not so much because they are Thomists (which has, in any case, been questioned), but because they have brought some of the insights of modern and contemporary philosophical thought into the theological task. Most significant among these are Karl Rahner, from whose early work, *Hearers of the Word*,[4] the title of this present endeavor has been adapted, and Bernard Lonergan, on whose reflections the notion of foundational theology is dependent.[5] It should be emphasized at this point that these supplemental authors will be aids in developing some of Polanyi's insights; their thought as such does not form the basis of our investigation.

Having marked out the boundaries of our study, we may now briefly provide a glimpse of the direction we shall travel by considering first the destination. Our ultimate goal is to propose a schematic outline accounting for the methods operative in theological understanding. Such a proposal, however, demands at least two further clarifications. In the first place, not all would agree to what the term "theology" refers (if, indeed, they thought it could legitimately refer). In fact, theological claims may be, and have been, approached from perspectives as diverse as anthropology, psychology, sociology, history, and philosophy, in addition to whatever may be its own proper standpoint. And secondly, depending on how one faces the first question, any applicable method would be correspondingly altered.

If, for example, theology were conceived to be a historical discipline, bent on analyzing and elucidating a corpus of sacred canonical writings along with their classical commentaries, the appropriate method would be the criteria of historical scholarship. But as the "history of history" clearly shows, these criteria have changed. Thus the hermeneutical problem must be investigated. As soon as this is begun, however, theology cannot be *simply* a historical endeavor: interpretation is necessary for analysis. Eventually therefore a systematic exposition must be included in the theological task.

On the level of systematic presentation, moreover, the problem of method becomes heightened, for here *the specifically theological form of understanding* comes to the fore. The medieval *quaestiones disputatae* are classic examples presupposing this form of understanding. Their purpose, according to St. Thomas Aquinas, was

> less to push error out than to lead listeners into the truth they strive to understand. Accordingly they must be carried by reasonings in order to get to the root of the matter, and helped to see for themselves how what is asserted is true. Otherwise, if the appeal is to merely bare authorities, then all the teacher does is to certify to his listeners that such in fact is the answer to the problem; apart from this they have gathered no reason for it and no understanding, and so go empty away.[6]

Just what are these "reasonings" which will get the inquirer "to the root of the matter" so that he will "understand" and not "go empty away"?

It is clear that when theology is held to be the systematic, theoretic explication of a community's faith, the problem of theological method must be explored at the foundational level. It would not be sufficient, for instance, to indicate how the systematic endeavor must be done in accordance with the findings of historical scholarship, while at the same time exerting its own influence by providing certain insights to aid in the task of clarifying the sources. Rather, the very possibility[7] of doing theology on the systematic level must be clarified. Only consequent to this task can there be any legitimate attempt at a systematic exposition.

This, then, is the meaning of "foundational theology" intended here. It is the attempt to found the theological enterprise through a radical description and explanation of the way we know.

In order to achieve this ultimate goal, we must begin with an analysis of human knowing. For this task we shall follow the lead of Michael Polanyi. Many of the component elements of Polanyi's reflections become more understandable when they are set in perspective by what may be termed his primary motivating force: This is Polanyi's conviction that critical reason and its concomitant passion for "objectivity" in knowing have hidden assumptions which are self-contradictory. *A critique of critical reason is thus called for*. Exposing such commonly held assumptions will allow us to proceed in the analysis of human knowing without being bound by any of their unwarranted claims.

Following this we shall then provide an introductory presentation of the basic elements of knowing, including the tacit dimension. After this is outlined and clarified, a way of validating knowledge must be proposed. Personal decisions must be capable of being sustained by valid affirmations if one is not to fall into subjectivism. The use of words, the meanings intended by the user, and their reliability for understanding reality will have to be clarified. All of this takes place within a context that is open and progressing. In man it is historical. This movement and its justification must be developed.

These investigations will enable us to turn next to that which we know: reality. Through the disclosure of the structure of tacit knowing, we shall find ourselves related to a multi-dimensional reality. No level is reducible in an intelligible way to a lower level. This correspondence between the structure of knowing ahd the levels of reality opens us to the panorama of the logic of emergence, where reality is understood and revealed to us in ever new ways. Knowledge is thus the discovery of intelligibility on our part and at the same time submission to what is there, leading eventually to our dwelling in it.

Man's historically constituted knowledge provides him access to reality; his community of faith provides access to transcendent reality. Based on his mode of knowing, this access must also be historical. We shall thus find that the meaning of faith, derived from the tradition in which the believer dwells, is still only fragmentary. In this sense it is partially analogous to a novice's understanding of theoretical physics. It is only partially analogous, however, because the novice may progress to the point where he comprehends the meaning of his discipline. The logic of emergence will show, on the other hand, that we can comprehend intelligibly only that which constitutes our level of being (including the levels below, of course). This means that the meaning of religious belief cannot be comprehended by man with full intelligibility.

Thus any meaning which religious belief may have must come from a source beyond man and can be understood only by partaking of that source. Since man is still on his way toward attaining that point, "God" remains for us as one unknown. The situation here is somewhat analogous to the attempt to analyze human life as a "machine." Certain valid insights and benefits are derived from relying on this model, but that which is specifically human escapes this form of intelligibility. Similarly we shall find that only by dwelling in a religious community will faith enable us to live by a form of understanding not yet fully intelligible to us. Finally, these clarifications will allow us to outline the kind of understanding theology seeks and to indicate briefly the way in which theology tries to achieve this.

NOTES TO CHAPTER I

1. Michael Polanyi, *The Tacit Dimension* (Garden City, N.Y.: Doubleday & Company, Inc., Anchor Books, 1967), p. 4. For the sake of brevity, subsequent references to Polanyi's writings will be cited, after the initial entry, by title alone.

2. Polanyi, *Personal Knowledge: Towards a Post-Critical Philosophy* (New York: Harper & Row, Publishers, Torch-book edition, 1964), ch. 4.

3. See, for example, *The Tacit Dimension*, p. 92.

4. Karl Rahner, *Hearers of the Word*, trans. by M. Richards (New York: Herder & Herder, 1969).

5. Lonergan's long-awaited book, *Method in Theology*, has just been published and, unfortunately, was not available for our study. It would have been a particularly helpful resource for clarifying our ideas in the section, "Theology As Understanding," in Chapter V below. An indication of the intent of this work appeared earlier in "Functional Specialties in Theology," *Gregorianum*, L (1969), 485-505.

6. *Quaestiones quodlibetales* 4, 18 as quoted in the "Introduction" by Thomas Gilby to the *Summa Theologiae*, 1 (1a,1) (New York: McGraw-Hill Book Company, 1964), p. xxi. Polanyi makes a similar appraisal of the theological task as the attempt to undertsand: "Theology pursued as an axiomatization of the Christian faith has an important analytic task. Though its results can be understood only by practising Christians, it can greatly help them to understand what they are practising" (*Personal Knowledge*, p. 282).

7. As a cautionary note we wish to emphasize again that this does not involve the question whether or not any specific religious doctrine or tradition is objectively true. The "possibility" intended here is that, since there are in fact religious traditions making certain claims, the basis on which they make these claims and the meaning these claims intend are open to investigation. The point then becomes this: Can religious belief as such be substantiated, at least insofar as an intelligible explanation of it can be offered? Or is the experience on which the tradition has grown so utterly unique that the very attempt to clarify the basis of religious belief—because of the limitation of the human mind, for example—is a pointless venture?

CHAPTER II

THE CRITIQUE OF CRITICAL REASON

This inquiry into the foundations of religious belief has a goal similar to that of the author whose thought will be used in developing this program. Michael Polanyi, when faced with the crisis science was undergoing earlier this century concerning its foundations, resolved to meet this challenge.[1] Not unlike the theological problem we are here investigating, he found that the effort called for a radical examination and explanation of our knowing process.

In most of contemporary science, logical positivism, as the theoretical explanation of its foundations, no longer enjoys the prestige it did thirty years ago. Nothing, however, seems to have taken its place. Polanyi notes, for instance, Ernest Nagel's 1961 account of science in *The Structure of Science*. In it Nagel admits that we do not know whether or not the current premises of science are true, and furthermore that if we tried to justify them we would find most of the premises doubtful. "In effect," Polanyi explains, "Nagel implies that we must save our belief in the truth of scientific explanations by refraining from asking what they are based upon."[2] Such a view, which holds that science does not need or is not capable of any sort of philosophical justification, may be a carry-over from the earlier era of positivism. But whatever the reason, unless we wish "to reduce modern physics to a sort of mystic chant over an unintelligible Universe,"[3] the problem of the human mode of knowing must be examined.

In order to achieve an understanding of science both explanatory and capable of justifying the endeavor, Polanyi discovered that he had to modify the commonly accepted notion of knowledge, which in turn had implications far beyond the

domains of science as such.[4] Accordingly, if we are to develop
a way of doing theology based on Polanyi's thought, we must
first examine the ideal of knowledge, along with some of its
implications, which Polanyi rejected. Against this backdrop
Polanyi's thought progressed and through it our understanding
of his thought should become clearer.

A. *The Ideal of Total Objectivity*

Western man has labored under a conception of knowledge
that has demanded complete and total objectivity. This is, of
course, a generalization. One might wish to recognize figures
such as Augustine or Kierkegaard who in various ways reacted
against this ideal. But the significant point is that they did
so within a framework of this ideal and have not offered a viable alternative. Thus while one may have looked for "the
really real" or "the clear and distinct idea," or rebelled
against this and insisted that "subjectivity is truth," the
ideal as such had remained constant.[5]

The rise of modern science, moreover, has instilled a
methodical rigor into this ideal. Now not only was the knowledge to be explicit and objective, but also the very means for
achieving this knowledge were precisely set forth. Everything
that was to be known about the world could now be known through
exact operations, open to all for verification, and could be
expressed in unequivocal language. This was implicit in the
Newtonian world-machine and was explicitly proffered by Laplace.

A key element in this method is its critical stance. Whatever could not stand the test of some criterion, usually empirical, was rejected as dogmatism. At its best, this critical
stance paved the way for genuine advances by clearing away some
cherished authoritative, but unfounded, assumptions. But when
left unchecked, it led the way to radical scepticism and chal-
lenged the very foundations of knowledge.

While this ideal of completely objective and detached
knowledge with its critical spirit has been predominant in the
sciences, it has managed to permeate and affect all intellectual endeavors. To the extent that a particular discipline was
able to emulate physics, to that extent was it deemed successful. One need only recall the origin of the social sciences

or the difficulty biologists encounter when they attempt to introduce the notion of "life" into their science in order to see the point.

Within this context, finally, a dichotomy has arisen. If, on the one hand, the stress is placed on that which is factual in an empirical sense, all else that man experiences devolves to the realm of the non-cognitive. If, on the other hand, the meaningfulness of the concretely existing individual's experience is stressed, all that which is *merely* fact becomes absurd. These poles of positivism and existentialism both agree to and uphold this fact/value dichotomy, though obviously from different perspectives and for different reasons.[6] As a result of the ideal of completely objective knowledge, value (since it must be conceived as essentially subjective in this context) can no longer qualify as an object of knowledge.

This has effectively meant that religious thought had to accept the status of being non-cognitive, or else assume a quasi-fundamentalist position by accepting revelation as an empirical datum and working from there. This is exemplified, in the case of the former, by Liberal Theology, the Modernist movement, and in the theology of Rudolf Bultmann; and, in the case of the latter, it is exemplified in much of conservative Roman Catholic thought and in the theology of Karl Barth.

Such, in brief, is the dilemma[7] of human knowledge as analyzed by Polanyi, along with an indication of its implication for utterances about religious belief. In the course of his attempt to provide an alternative view of knowledge which is able to overcome this dilemma, Polanyi has pointed to a fundamental logical difficulty and to some further consequences that result from holding to an ideal of complete objectivity. After presenting Polanyi's critique of this ideal, we shall be in a favorable position to provide a preliminary sketch of Polanyi's own understanding of the human mode of knowing.

B. *The Logical Impossibility of the Ideal of Total Objectivity*

In order for anything to count as "objective" knowledge there must be a set of data which can be interpreted rather rigorously by some set method, thereby minimizing the subject's capacity for distortion. And in order for this knowledge to be

totally objective, the subject would have to be completely detached and would have to have a set of data capable of explaining all of nature.

With the rise of modern science men began to feel that
they were now capable of such a feat. Thanks to the analytic
rigor of the empirical method and Newton's synthetic representation of results achieved up to that time, man's hopes ran
high. Laplace's formulation of ideal science in absolute detachment, where a Universal Mind would possess a knowledge of
the location of all particles of nature and their interacting
forces and would then be able to compute everything past and
present, is perhaps the most explicit formulation of this
ideal.[8] But whether formulated or not, some such understanding of the nature and function of science and, more generally,
knowledge has held sway throughout the modern era.

A close scrutiny of this ideal of totally objective knowledge reveals, however, that it cannot possibly be achieved.
The fact that the ideal nevertheless has succeeded in capti-
vating men's minds up to the present can only be accounted for,
according to Polanyi,[9] by the hidden assumption whereby the
suppposed Universal Mind would tacitly supply meaning to the
observed and computed data. This is the fallacy of every reductive explanation when it claims to explain objectively such
things as man, art, or religion: it must first assume the
thing it is explaining. Yet the assumption is more than the
claim allows. In order for it to have the semblance of validity, the ideal of totally objective knowledge must make a subtle substitution of our knowledge of physics for our knowledge
of all other experiences as well. "Once you refuse this deceptive substitution, you immediately see that the Laplacean mind
understands precisely nothing and that whatever it knows means
precisely nothing."[10]

This fallacy can be illustrated even more clearly by means
of the relationship of physics and chemistry to engineering.
Polanyi often makes use of this example in his argument against
reductive schemes.[11] The salient feature of this illustration
is that it shows that the ideal of totally objective knowledge
cannot be validly applied to certain entities even though the
frame of reference remains on the inanimate level.

Thus let us imagine a machine--such as a typewriter--which has been subjected to an exhaustive physical and chemical analysis. And let us next suppose that we have the results of this analysis before us: a set of charts and mathematical formulae describing the complete physical and chemical makeup of the typewriter. Such information would be totally worthless if our concern was identifying what these elements composed or what purpose their joint constitution served. In short, this completely "objective" knowledge of the typewriter could not tell us that we were dealing with a typewriter. "So it follows that the Laplacean Mind would be subject to the same limitation: it could not identify any machine nor tell us how it works. Indeed, the Laplacean Mind could identify no object or process, the meaning of which consists in serving a purpose."[12] Needless to say, the difficulty is only compounded when such items as life, man, or history are introduced.[13]

By shifting our focus now to the demand for clearly explicit formulations in this ideal of totally objective knowledge, we can see further its incapacity to account for some traditional philosophical problems, specifically the problem of universals and discovery. This does not underscore the fallacy of the completely objectivist framework as did the above analysis by Polanyi, but it does indicate some of its characteristic weaknesses.

The fact that we do apply class concepts to things quite regularly and (almost invariably) accurately and that these things are varied in their particulars has never been satisfactorily explained by Western thought. The reason for this, in Polanyi's understanding, is the demand for absolute clarity in specifying how we come to know and use universals and the attempt to eliminate the indeterminate elements involved in recognizing a particular instance as a member of a class. This attempt Polanyi feels is misguided.[14] Only when we remove ourselves from the grasp of an objectivist framework can we understand the legitimacy of our use of universal terms.

A similar difficulty manifests itself in the problem of discovery. This is particularly surprising in light of the fact that science itself thrives on discovery. Yet, while scientists continually do their work and propose their creative innovations, philosophers have been unable to provide the precise canons that would account for this. Indeed, the inductive process as such provides only degrees of probability and what items or data are to be taken into account in this process are hardly specifiable at all.

Polanyi's diagnosis finds that the cause of this difficulty lies in the demand for absolute clarity and the complete explicitness of knowledge. The problem of providing a totally explicit account of the process of discovery has accordingly been present since the beginnings of Western thought. According to Polanyi's interpretation, it is precisely this assumption that leads to the paradox of discovery uncovered by Plato in the *Meno*.[15] If all knowledge is explicit, then we could never truly discovery anything new. Without having the slightest clue as to what we were looking for we could not discover it even if we chanced to come across it. In Polanyi's estimation, then, Plato indirectly demonstrated in his *Meno* "that if problems nevertheless exist, and discoveries can be made by solving them, we can know things, and important things, that we cannot tell."[16] Again it is only when we remove ourselves from an objectivist framework that we may begin to appreciate our valid ability to make genuine discoveries.

For Polanyi the most significant consequences resulting from the ideal of totally objective knowledge are not primarily the realization that it rests upon assumptions which are logically self-defeating, nor simply that such an ideal falters in explaining factors in the everyday experience of most men. In addition to this, and in Polanyi's estimation far more serious, are the consequences that flow from this ideal when it is used as a guide to understanding specifically human affairs.

C. *Some Consequences of Holding to the Ideal of Total Objectivity*

The preceding discussion has outlined Polanyi's reasons for rejecting the ideal of knowledge that would demand complete objectification and detachment in a critical spirit. The ideal, insofar as it is seemingly embodied in the scientific endeavor, is dominating our civilization. This means that, in addition to these theoretical difficulties which have been uncovered,

this tendency is obviously having other effects beyond that of
a way of conceiving the nature of science. Here much more serious consequences result, for as Polanyi points out, "these
false ideals do no harm to physicists, who only pay lip service
to them, but they play havoc with other parts of science and
with our whole culture, which try to live by them."[17] In order
to understand this pervasive influence, it will be helpful to
illustrate this mechanism as it has been traditionally set
forth for the physical sciences before we look at the impact
it has had on our cultural milieu.

If one were to attempt to characterize the prevailing mood
of the scientific enterprise, it could be done by describing
the task of science as a coherent description of experience.
This means that a particular natural phenomenon is regarded as
a scientific "fact" insofar as it is a manifestation of some
general pattern or "law." Furthermore these general explanations have as their purpose the desire to "simplify" or make
more manageable our dealings with natural phenomena, thereby
making competing descriptions alternative ways of doing the
same thing; but usually one of these varying descriptions is
chosen by the scientific community because it is the most con-
venient (or "simplest") way of dealing with any particular set
of phenomena of our experience. The question as to whether
these explanations are "real" or "true" is ignored, because,
it is supposed, the method does not allow such "metaphysical
speculations" to arise legitimately.[18]

The rationale for adopting this stance is to reduce as
much as possible the personal or "psychological" factor brought
into the picture by the scientist himself. As we have seen in
the previous section, this led to the attempt to view science
(and implicitly all knowledge) as a factual or objective mode
of inquiry, while more subjective or value-laden judgments
were reserved to other modes of appreciation or feeling.[19]
The result is a circular and self-justifying pattern which continually strives for greater objectification by appealing to
experience at the expense of the personal involvement of the
practicing scientist.

When this emphasis on factual experience was pushed to its
extreme formulation earlier in this century, scientific theories

were so intimately linked with such "objective" experience that
a scientist was expected to drop any theory the moment some
factual observation conflicted with it. The pervasive hold
that this view still has on our popular culture can be illustrated by the not uncommon expression of surprise that registers
on the faces of undergraduate students when they are told that
the idea "that a scientist immediately drops a hypothesis the
moment it conflicts with evidence is a pure myth."[20]

A similar expectation is manifested in the contention that
any new scientific development is only a "working hypothesis"
which will be eventually replaced when new facts so warrant.
To this point Polanyi makes the following observation:

> This. . .is either meaningless or untrue. If it
> means that a scientific proposition is abandoned
> whenever some new observation is accepted as evi-
> dence against it, then the statement is, of course,
> tautologous. If it suggests that any new obser-
> vation which formally contradicts a proposition
> leads to its abandonment, it is, equally obviously,
> false.[21]

Thus to call a scientific theory a "working hypothesis" in the
first sense is to make a vacuous claim. But more important for
our purpose is the recognition that if this is taken literally
in the second sense, it is a false way of understanding scientific development.

The primary reason for this concerns the assumption of the
mechanical and automatic application and correlation of scientific theories and canons with experience. This automatic,
indeed blind, application is impossible to achieve in practice.
When to dismiss the result of a particular experiment which
seems to contradict prevailing scientific views as an inadequate experiment, or to set it aside temporarily as an anomaly,
or to pursue it vigorously as a significant achievement which
may qualify it to overturn prevailing scientific models--all
these require judgments which no explicit set of scientific
norms or rules will ever specify. And this means then that
values of some sort are involved even in some of the most trivial of scientific activities.

This now means we have come full circle from the commonly
accepted understanding of science. Polanyi holds that every
scientist shares a set of premisses[22] or accepts a paradigm[23]

which functions as a context, normally inarticulate, within which scientists do their work and apply their explicit criteria.

This is illustrated in subtle manner, even if we were to look at the way a typical case of verification is analyzed according to the common understanding of science. What is generally chosen as an example of verification by textbooks is not at all in question. Thus what is really being illustrated by the example is a practical demonstration of a law, not its critical verification. The predominant view of science, in short, by trying to discount the scientist's acceptance of a set of premises and his personal judgments within it effectively blocks out genuine verification.[24]

That the personal judgment of the scientist is of prime importance and goes beyond simple explicit rules is made even more manifest when the failures of scientists are considered, particularly when practical consequences follow. When such failures occur, the scientist is normally judged imcompetent or at least to have acted poorly in the situation. Appeal to the proper execution of scientific rules cannot justify his mistake. "The scientist's task is not to observe any allegedly correct procedure but to get the right results."[25]

Contained in such an appraisal of scientific activity is the notion that science deals with reality, however this term be understood. The contention of much speculation earlier this century on the purpose of science regarding this point seems very strange today. Consider, for example, Poincare's critique of Galileo's claim for the reality of the heliocentric theory, or Duhem's further claim that the adversaries of the Copernicans were the ones who truly understood the nature of scientific assertions![26] While this has unquestionably been the predominant view of science, it is very likely correct to say that today it is changing.[27] Those who practiced science firsthand probably were never fully spellbound by the traditional view--at least not in the practice of their profession. Nevertheless the traditional notions about science have been around for so long that they are still exercizing profound authority. This is true both with respect to the life sciences and to culture in general.

For quite some time there has been a growing recognition of our inability to deal with that which we consider characteristically human. For example, as early as 1931 Pierre Teilhard de Chardin remarked that "man in his essential characteristics has been omitted from all scientific theories of nature."[28] This lack of adequate conceptual tools, unfortunately, still permeates our culture, and its effects are to be seen surrounding us everywhere. Technology has advanced at a pace bewildering to us. We do not know how to use it; so much so that man has practically become its servant. Of all that is still mysterious to us in the world, our own self-understanding probably ranks highest. In fact the very way we think and live in the world we have created will usually prevent such a question about ourselves from even arising in our consciousness. If, in some unguarded moment, we do begin to wonder what our place in this maze we call Western Civilization is, we are inclined by our cultural setting either to dismiss the question as meaningless or perhaps to set the "real world out there" aside temporarily while we spend some time reflecting on this "religious" question the next time we go to church.

Even though these lines may be considered overdrawn, it nevertheless remains true that the possibilities for authentically understanding man are marginal if we try to remain at the same time scientific. Here one of the major contentions of Polanyi becomes clearly visible. The dominating hold of traditional conceptions of scientific knowledge is one of the primary contributing factors to this Western schizophrenia.

Historically the basis for this was laid by Cartesian dualism, followed up by Newton's incorporation of mechanistic atomism into his scientific world-view. Reality was now "inert"--a basic assumption for the applicability of Newtonian science. As time went on the "spiritual" qualities that may have been once deemed necessary for understanding life, particularly human life, were dropped from sight. Such assumptions were no longer necessary to explain things scientifically. In the last resort it became commonly accepted that a reductivist scheme was sufficient to explain everything. As a result the Cartesian-Newtonian world-machine was devoid of life.[29]

Nor has this conclusion been effectively changed by the

revolutionary insights of Darwin. "On the contrary," Dr.
Majorie Grene remarks,

> what was so triumphantly successful in Darwin's
> theory was precisely its reduction of life to the
> play of chance and necessity, its elimination of
> organic categories from the interpretation even of
> living things. True, modern Darwinians are at-
> tempting, in a confused and confusing way, to deny,
> or to rectify, this reductive tendency; the fact
> remains that Darwinism as a comprehensive theory
> is reductive, and still essentially Cartesian, in
> its interpretation of the organic world. Not, in-
> deed, nature in the eighteenth century sense, not
> nature as a machine, but nature as a mechanically
> interacting aggregate of machines: that is the
> Darwinian vision.[30]

The model of evolution here assumes that whatever is evolving
is to be taken univocally and minimally. There are no permis-
sible categories which would allow for development in the sense
of "emergence" of "higher" forms. The meaning of development
instead becomes modification through chance variations (as in
the arrangement of genes) and necessary natural selection over
a period of many generations (by eliminating less well adapted
variants through environmental forces). Modern biology has,
for the most part, moved within such a lifeless circle.[31]

Thus as a result of the commonly accepted scientific para-
digm--in the sense used earlier--biologists cannot deal with
those phenomena which seemingly would be of primary interest,
namely living organisms and purposive behavior.[32] There simply
is no valid way of accounting for such factors, since any hierarchically conceived categories and any teleological assumptions
have to be brought in from the outside. If they are brought in
out of some recognition of an inadequacy in the existing framework, such notions simply "hang" without any logical network
connecting them within the discipline. In short, argues Polanyi, the predominant view of biology has a note about it that
seems to be false in terms of our experience. Moreover, it is
in fact impossible to carry out an objectivist type of biological study in practice as we have seen above.

These considerations clarify greatly the reasons why man
himself would be problematic for modern science. In the perspective of Polanyi's analysis, it is not at all surprising
that man, as seen through current scientific conceptions, is

a sophisticated automaton, for "a strict behaviorism is the logical terminus of looking at man in a completely detached manner, in accordance with the accepted ideal of the scientific method."[33] Learning becomes a series of random responses to external conditions which eventually and fortuitously hits upon a correct response, thereby enabling the subject to repeat the response upon the experience of similar conditions. A completely objectivist and mechanical model of learning is thus thought to be provided. Yet it makes tacit assumptions unwarranted by its stated aims. A behaviorist theory can only exploit very crude models of learning, for in complex situations the recognition of repeated states of affairs and the decision to adopt a previously learned response call for a discrimination that no formal inductive system has ever been able to specify.[34]

Further, since the intent of this type of an approach is to rule out any dealings with categories beyond those empirically observable--that is, categories such as "mind," "person," or "evaluation"--the logical, but strange, conclusion is drawn that such things as "persons" (insofar as they intend to refer to a reality in itself) are not real. Or, as Gilbert Ryle has put it, "overt intelligent performances are not clues to the workings of minds; they are those workings."[35] By accepting the reigning paradigm of objectivity and by not wishing to fall into Cartesian dualism, Ryle logically denies the reality of "mind." Yet this analysis suffers from the same flaws as the typical behaviorist models of learning. In and of themselves, particular acts of some "mind" would be meaningless unless observed from a larger context of pointing to the reality of someone performing them; and this in turn implies that we do not focus on the "workings" directly, but only insofar as we subsidiarily assume them to be manifestations of some person's mind, which is what we know primarily.[36]

At this point an objection could be raised about the validity of Polanyi's analysis. If his appraisal has some merit, then why have so many been held under the sway of an objectivist framework? That is, what has prevented behaviorists, for example, from uncovering their supposed inconsistency? Ultimately an attempt to answer this brings us to the central nexus

of Polanyi's position and can only be justified by the argument
as it unfolds throughout this work. For the time being it will
perhaps suffice to note that our articulate framework, like the
air we breathe, engulfs us, and we rarely, if ever, notice it.
"Our most ingrained convictions," Polanyi writes,

> are determined by the idiom in which we interpret our
> experience and in terms of which we erect our arti-
> culate systems. Our formally declared beliefs can be
> held to be true in the last resort only because of
> our logically anterior acceptance of a particular
> set of terms, from which all our references to real-
> ity are constructed.37

The problem thus lies at this logically anterior threshold, not
within the behaviorist or the Polanyian positions in themselves.
And here is precisely the heart of the matter: an objectivist
view cannot allow such a problematic, for by so doing it would
in this very admission cease to be objectivist. In short, an
objectivist view would have to admit the personal involvement
of the knower in the knowing process through which he structures his reference to reality.

Such a move to a new articulate framework which would acknowledge personal ideals has been effectively forestalled by
the objectivist mentality through a subterfuge Polanyi calls
"pseudo-substitution." This is a practice

> used to play down man's real and indispensible in-
> tellectual powers for the sake of maintaining an
> "objectivist" framework which in fact cannot account
> for them. It works by defining scientific merit in
> terms of its relatively trivial features, and making
> these function in the same way as the true terms
> which they are supposed to replace.38

If we return for a moment to the behavioristic theory of learning, the significance of this criticism will become clearer.
We have already seen how the examples of learning which are
used are very simple ones. Moreover there is an ambiguity in
the "impersonal" terms which allows the observer to supply
implicitly to the activity components which the terms themselves fail to include. A "stimulus" and a "response" are so
only in a context which supplies meaning and value, an implied
"rightness." Taken literally, such objectivist terms would not
talk about "learning" at all. Because the experimenter tacitly
supplies meaning to otherwise random activity, the "open

texture" of words such as stimulus seemingly work. But they
function no better (actually worse, Polanyi is arguing) than
the mentalistic terms they are thought to replace.[39] The same
things holds true with the scientific enterprise itself. A
term such as "simplicity" is used in place of a more personal
term such as the "rationality" of a theory.[40] Even the critical stance itself has been subsumed into this network. What
is it that science doubts? Certainly not everything. Only
those things are to be doubted which should be reasonably
doubted. But what constitutes reasonable doubt? Nothing we
could explicitly formulate would ever cover the range of valid
applications of a rule of doubt. Scientists' implicit beliefs
spill over to allow a seemingly objectivist appraisal of doubt
to operate in practice.[41]

A logical corollary of this whole movement led to the
denial of human values--at least insofar as they might be explicitly professed. The idiom of scientific thinking had so
dehumanized our perception of reality that even the most commonly held values had to be transformed into some sort of technical and objectifiable language. Polanyi has described this
process in very caustic terms:

> Indeed, by leave of the sociologist it will become
> once more respectable to know good and evil, and
> even to love the one and hate the other, provided
> only you always remember to express yourself de-
> cently in scientific terms. The public, which has
> learned to distrust its traditional morality, is
> only too happy to receive its substance back from
> the sociologist's hand in a scientifically branded
> wrapping.[42]

So long as the moral values which these scientific expressions
are attempting to replace are implicitly retained, such a
pseudo-substitution may actually allow these moral values to
function--and to function well enough to effect significant
reform as in the cases of Bentham and Dewey.[43] When this is
the result, however, the replacement of moral ideals by scientific expressions is primarily verbal. Effective restraints
in the society prevent this from being fully realized. This is
especially true in England and the United States, because their
strong religious traditions and their long history of democratic
civic institutions operated as hidden forces throughout the

period of the liberal-scientific era.[44]

Thus the critical-objectivist movement begun during the period of the Enlightenment ended the dominance of ecclesiastical institutions and particularly their hold on the intellectual frameworks in moral matters. The moral values aroused by Christianity nevertheless spilled over into secular culture. As we have indicated, this led to many immediate reforms and developments in social conditions. But what happens when there are no effective restraints holding in check the critical spirit? Or what happens when the desire for critical lucidity is overcome by the moral drives it has unleashed? Here the most serious and damaging consequence of the critical-objectivist framework is brought to light: modern man has been torn between these two pressing but ever more obviously conflicting ideals--critical objectivity and moral perfection. As they have become ingrained in his cultural life in the course of time, they have also fused into various combinations which were inherently unstable because they were at bottom self-contradictory.

This process has led to a state of affairs Polanyi calls "moral inversion."[45] By means of this intellectual construct Polanyi proposes both a conceptual tool for analyzing modern ethical movements and an interpretation of political theories. It is thus useful for examining two otherwise unrelated tendencies in the modern world, namely the absolute individuality of men leading in its extreme expression to nihilism and the absolute authority of the state for the good of all leading in its extreme expression to totalitarianism. Both of these movements are the logical terminus, though with differing emphases, of a moral inversion.

The personal variant of this phenomenon, like its political counterpart, may be described as a hidden moral sensitivity operating through an openly declared immorality. The focus here is different, but the underlying dynamics are similar. The search for critical lucidity relegated morality to materialistic interpretations. Yet when this was seen as unsatisfactory because of the quest for objectivity and intellectual honesty, this was consistently pressed to its extreme breaking point and as a result a flood of moral passion was let loose in the name of social or personal goals that were felt to be capable of immediate achievement. On the personal level this has led to nihilism and modern day existentialism. The Russian intellectuals of the 1860's, Nietzsche, Diderot, Rousseau were all historical examples of this state. Today scepticism and moral perfectionism combine to attack all explicit expressions of morality. A state exists where men driven by implicit moral passions attack morality. This is the protean existential man, making himself in the face of a totally objective and absurd world. He is Saint Genet--in his absolute demands for authentically being himself he openly flaunts traditional morality lest he succomb to the anguish of bad faith. This brings on the paradoxical and inherently unstable situation of moral righteousness filled with contempt for its overt expression. By denying their ideals, moral passions can then only be expressed through a nihilism turned against itself.[46]

In what sense we may ask, however, is it valid to suppose that the individual must assume absolute responsibility for himself by becoming the sole criterion for his every action? In the face of a complex and ever changing reality, this is impossible. Any statement about reality or any real act, should the subject demand absolute moral clarity, can be nothing more than an expression of bad faith. Critical lucidity when pushed in this direction effectively makes the world absurd and reduces the knowing subject to nothing, a chasm in being. The only basis for such an existentialist description of the human condition resides in the prior assumption that all knowledge must be explicit.[47] But if Polanyi's insight that we dwell in a non-explicit *cognitive* framework is understood, the existential choice facing men is no longer set within a dichotomy of absolute self-determination seeking perfection and an absurd world opaque to our demands for clarity. Rather, the actual concrete existence of the historically situated being is upheld along with the assumptions that make him and allow him to go beyond himself and his milieu in a genuine way. In this way the "alienated man" is seen as the abstraction it is, in spite of its "existential" pretensions.

Alongside this individualistic form of moral inversion, a political variant developed which exhibited a similar underlyin

dynamic process,[48] even though it arrived at the opposite conclusion: the suppression of the individual for the sake of
the state. Here the process operates by satisfying the boundless demands for moral perfection that exist in the modern
world through an expression of these ideals covertly in an objective guise. This is the major reason for the success of
Marxism.[49] By interpreting history in a manner reminiscent of
Laplace, that is, as a scientifically mechanistic interplay of
forces of power and economics, it satisfied the demand for critical lucidity. At the same time it gave full play to the moral demands of its adherents by assuring them that their desire
for social progress was the inevitable result of the historical
process. Utopia is transformed into a science, one that demands and sanctions any sort of action to achieve its aim and
effectively cuts off moral criticism by attacking the critic's
non-scientific and "emotive" character.

It should thus be clear that to accuse Marxism of "materialism" is to miss the point; its scientific materialism is
used to cover up its moral dynamism. Likewise to criticize
Marxism in logical terms results in failure because this approach does not take into account the tacit moral aspirations
that give life to the scientific theory. As a result of such
a "dynamo-objective coupling,"[50] this form of moral inversion
not only is able to satisfy the modern demand for critical objectivity and high moral resolve, it is also able to come to
its own defense through a self-confirming circle. The objective, scientific aspect brushes aside moral critiques and its
underlying moral dynamism enables it to reject theoretical
criticism. This explains, to some extent at least, why typical religious condemnations of Marxism on moral grounds are
usually fruitless (consider the case of Italy) and why typical
academic expositions of the logical fallacy in working for a
cause already determined do not undermine the attraction for
Marxism (consider many college radicals).

As a result of this transposition of moral concerns into
scientific garb, much more serious consequences result than a
simple self-deception on the part of the holders. By being
wrenched from their moral context, the moral motives underlying
Marxism become isolated and, since they are free from moral

criticism or restraint, fanatical. The major thrust of Polanyi's analysis, moreover, contends that such moral inversion is
not limited to the processes, however frequent or infrequent,
of political injustices. Rather, like its existential counterpart, it leads to a state where the very conception of "reality" and "truth" is altered.

We can see now what Polanyi means when he contends that
he developed his theory of personal knowledge in response to
the Marxist conception of truth and reality as applied to science and how this in turn led him to the critique of the ideal
of knowledge developed during the modern era because the then
prevailing positivist view of science was impotent to meet
another opposing conception.[51] This may be concretely illustrated from Polanyi's personal experiences with Bukharin in
1935. Three years before his own execution, Bukharin argued
that "pure science" was a bourgeois myth and that in a class-
less society all science would work automatically according to
the dictates of the state.[52] Another more telling example of
how the dogma of the party affects the conceptions of reality
and truth is the notorious Lysenko affair, where graduate
students working in genetics were told: "You don't have to
work in true scientific fashion. Just prove Lysenko right."[53]

Even more startling is the effect this had on some of the
staunchest supporters of the revolution. If in fact the scientific social theory *is* reality, then there is no place for such
notions as "truth" independent of the party. Bukharin thus
lied and condemned himself, for to tell the truth would have
been to condemn the revolution. Perhaps even more striking was
the case of Arthur London, the Czech socialist. The dramatic
events of his arrest and confession to various crimes against
the state recorded in his memoir were such that a movie was
made of them. Considering his ability to withstand the horrors
of a Nazi death camp and his past record of party loyalty, one
is led to wonder how or even why he would confess. In viewing
the film version of this event, a critic expressed the following thoughts on the matter:

> Through the whole affair London remained the
> one thing he'd always been above all else: a loyal
> Party member and a dedicated Marxist. As a Marxist
> he believed that individual freedom requires con-

sciousness of historical necessity. To recognize
the inevitable is to be liberated by it: that's
dogma. But such paradoxical Marxism has always run
the risk of being practiced as double-think. What
if the dictatorship of the proletariate can only
advance through a purge of the Party's Jews? What
if historical necessity should require a man to tell
self-incriminating lies? Must not the man then
achieve freedom by resigning himself to imprisonment?

Having raised these questions in his mind,
London's interrogators let his own feelings of guilt
and self-doubt about his dedication to the Party do
the rest. He worked on himself morally from the in-
side while they worked on him physically and psycho-
logically from the outside. But the crucial conflict
was the interior one. The State could only prey on
that conflict and exploit its final resolution. The
Party didn't turn on London despite his past loyalty,
but *because of* it. His loyalty made him the ideal
victim, and a more able accomplice to his own ruin-
ation than any false witness could have been. By
isolating him on the level of consciousness to
which history and his own efforts doomed him, the
Party did to him what the Nazis could never do.54

Here are the ideals of objectivity and moral perfection run a-
ground and attacking the very thirst for truth that first set
these ideals loose during the Enlightenment.

While these political and nihilistic forms of moral inversion may be the most devastating consequence of the ideal
of totally objective knowledge, Polanyi does not wish his analysis to be taken to imply that modern Western conceptions of
politics have not been affected by this ideal. Much of what
passes for democratic idealism is, by means of a pseudo-substitution, nothing more than crass self-interest on the part of
Western nations. Moreover the academic schools of value-free
sociology or political science are undoubtedly the predominant
ones. It is not unusual to hear questions like "What is the
common good?" branded as remnants of "political theology." And
so when Western theorists are faced with events like the Hungarian and Polish uprisings of 1956 or the Czechoslovakian developments up to 1968, they act like their Marxist counterparts
in assuming there must be some "objective" or "scientific" external data which account for these phenomena. To hold that
the intellectuals in these countries were moved by a search
for "truth" is regarded as "naive and unscientific."55 But
this is in fact the reason given by those involved. What is

needed in the West is a political theory which not only takes
into account values, but regards them as integral constituents
of its methodology.[56] Only when this is accomplished will the
spell of total objectivity be broken in this area.

But this is still not enough. How can this ideal of totally objective knowledge as such be altered? This is the basic question toward which the entire preceding analysis had
been tending. For if Polanyi is correct, then the many theoretical and cultural problems facing the West today will only
be resolved by admitting that our current conception of knowledge is inadequate and by beginning the quest for a new one.

D. *Knowledge as Personal*

The problem as it has been outlined from the Polanyian
perspective is that the demand for totally objective knowledge,
which has grown beyond all proportion in the modern and contemporary eras, has led us to the paradoxical position where
"truth," "reality," and "value" all have become problematic,
including the one who would be the subject of such knowledge,
namely "man." Insofar as any open-minded person has understood
the argument as it unfolded, he would have to admit that something is askew. It may be that Polanyi's analysis is invalid
in some way, in which case we may explain away the difficulties
he uncovers as being illusory or, if real, simply the way things
are. But the evidence he has brought forth to show that the
prevailing positivistic view of science, and by extension, all
knowledge, is at bottom logically self-contradictory and without foundation, that the resulting mechanistic and determinis-
tic underpinnings of most biological and psychological research
cannot deal with life and consciousness, that the social-scientific treatment of traditional ethical questions is done only
by means of a deceptive substitution, and finally that our desire for critical lucidity coupled with a boundless and home-
less moral passion has led to inversions which threaten the
very existence of Western culture--the evidence for all this
must make one pause.

On the other hand, if Polanyi's analysis is correct, as
the evidence would suggest, then it seems as if the fate of
despair is all that is left to man. Such an existential resig-

nation, however, is inadequate since it too is a result of the ideal of total objectivity. No, what is called for is nothing short of a complete change of perspective, a reorientation of our world, a conversion to a new horizon where the expression, "all knowledge is personal," articulates what we are and what we mean. Polanyi's "solution" to the quandary raised by the ideal of total objectivity is at once naively simple and profoundly revolutionary.

It is simple because it asks only that we recognize the personal activity involved in every act of knowledge. But this is revolutionary in its implications for it requires a readjustment of the way we normally see ourselves in the knowing process and the way we normally see the objects of our knowing. It demands, basically, that we understand man to be a person involved in a search, not for detached objectivity, but for *truth*, a truth which goes beyond his individual predispositions, yet which is not enveloped by the dictates of society.

Quite obviously, at this level of discussion "logic" and "objectivity" are not the points at issue, but the way in which objectivity and logic are viewed and the place they assume in one's overall perspective. This means, in turn, that there is no "proof" for the superiority of Polanyi's theory of personal knowledge as such. Rather, a sympathetic shift--even if only temporary and for the sake of continuing the discussion--to Polanyi's stance is necessary in order to be in a favorable position to judge the validity of his theory. The reason for this is that by making this move, a commitment, at least partial and perhaps still hesitant, is being entered into whereby one shares a view of reality with another. And such a shift cannot be "proven" in any normal sense of the term, because, as Polanyi points out, "you cannot formalize the act of commitment, for you cannot express your commitment non-committally."[57]

Usually, however, we would not be driven to question our non-articulate perspective which stresses objectivity and detachment (thereby attempting to imply that it is *not a* perspective, but *the* perspective), unless we first see some reason for doing so. The purpose of "The Critique of Critical Reason" was precisely to expose this need. Still, even if the seed of doubt concerning the ideal of total objectivity is now present,

we cannot proceed directly to a complete understanding of Polanyi's position. We must make our way gradually, learning of
it until it becomes a part of us. Again the reason for this
circuitous route in entering the horizon of thought developed
by Polanyi is that "it is. . .logically impossible for the human mind to divest itself of all uncritically acquired foundations. For our minds cannot unfold at all except by embrac-
ing a definite idiom of beliefs, which will inevitably determine the scope of our entire subsequent fiducial development."[58]
What we are attempting to do here is to shift idioms of beliefs,
not to argue logically within a particular idiom.

To clarify the dynamic isomorphism between our articulate
expressions and our inarticulate assumptions, Polanyi has developed a system of interrelated concepts that may be said to
describe the idiom of his thought. But immediately a note of
caution must be issued here because this system only serves to
"acquaint" the inquirer, as it were, with what is happening in
his acts of knowing and is not personal knowledge itself. As
we have seen above, the activity of research cannot be explicitly defined at all. "Like the rules of all other higher
arts, they are codified in practice alone."[59] The following
description must be taken as an invitation to explore the possibility of this range of experience in the reader's own conscious activity.

Briefly, then, we have arrived at the point where we can
see that the ideal of knowledge opting for critical lucidity
rendered much of everyday experience problematic and as a result we should be able to appreciate the fact that this ideal
has its inarticulate basis. From this point we may perhaps
move to a new perspective which tries to incorporate this inarticulate basis as a necessary element in the knowing process.
Both explicit expressions and the tacit bases out of which the
explicit statements are made constitute knowledge, though of
different kinds. The personal act of the knower then means
that "we always know tacitly that we are holding our explicit
knowledge to be true."[60] From such a vantage point, a whole
new panorama of reality emerges which is hierarchically ordered and value-laden. And if our analysis validates this as
a viable and acceptable expression of our cognitional activity,

it may likewise prove to be an adequate way of grounding religious belief and theological assertions.

32

NOTES TO CHAPTER II

1. See, for example, the Introduction to the 1964 edition of
    Science, Faith and Society (Chicago: University of Chi-
    cago Press, Phoenix books, 1964), pp. 7-19.

2. Michael Polanyi, "The Growth of Science in Society," in
    Knowing and Being, ed. by Marjorie Grene (Chicago: Uni-
    versity of Chicago Press, 1969), p. 73.

3. Alfred North Whitehead, *Modes of Thought* (New York:
    Capricorn Books, 1958), p. 185.

4. *Personal Knowledge*, p. xiii.

5. This assessment is based on Marjorie Grene's *The Knower
    and the Known* (London: Faber & Faber, 1966) in which
    she has defended this thesis through an appraisal of
    Aristotle, Plato, Descartes, and the rise of modern sci-
    ence--all in view of Polanyi's thought. See for example
    the following comment (p. 13): "Both the ideal of reason
    as analysis, in each of its guises and disguises, and
    the revolt against reason by more subjectivist philoso-
    phers, have remained, whether as acceptance or rebellion,
    within this single conceptual frame."

6. For a similar appraisal of the contemporary scene, see
    Jerry H. Gill, "The Tacit Structure of Religious Knowing,"
    International Philosophical Quarterly, IX (1969), 534 and
    Walter Kaufmann, *Critique of Religion and Philosophy* (New
    York: Harper & Brothers, Publishers, 1958).

7. Polanyi has elaborated this further in the context of
    his own thought as the "objectivist dilemma" (see *Per-
    sonal Knowledge*, p. 304ff), which, if we may anticipate,
    refuses to accredit the personal involvement of the
    knower, leaving a void between one's "subjective beliefs"
    and an actual state of affairs.

8. Polanyi notes that contemporary physics would modify this,
    but it does not effectively reduce its scope (*Personal
    Knowledge*, p. 140 n. 2).

9. *Personal Knowledge*, p. 140.

10. *Ibid.*, p. 141.

11. For a sampling of Polanyi's treatment of this point, see
    the following: "Life Transcending Physics and Chemistry,"
    Chemical and Engineering News, XLV (August 21, 1967), 54-
    66; in *Knowing and Being*, "Tacit Knowing: Its Bearing
    on Some Problems of Philosophy," pp. 159-180, "The
    Structure of Consciousness," pp. 211-224, and "Life's
    Irreducible Structure," pp. 225-239; *The Study of Man*
    (Chicago: University of Chicago Press, Phoenix Books,
    1963), "Lecture II"; and *The Tacit Dimension*, ch. 2.

12. *The Study of Man*, p. 49.

13. Lest this be misleading, it must be noted that Polanyi does not imply by this argument that entities, which have a purpose beyond that defined by physics, have no relationship to or dependence on their physical makeup. On the contrary, as we shall see, such entities are thoroughly dependent on physical and chemical laws. Polanyi's point here is simply that they cannot be accounted for solely by this means and the ideal of knowledge which implies they can is mistaken.

14. "Logic and Psychology," *American Psychologist*, XXIII (1968), 35-36. See also in *Knowing and Being*, "The Unaccountable Element in Science," pp. 105-106 and "Tacit Knowing: Its Bearing on Some Problems of Philosophy," pp. 165-168.

15. The relevant passage is 80D where Meno asks Socrates: "Why, on what lines will you look, Socrates, for a thing of whose nature you know nothing at all?" The context here is our knowledge of virtue, but Plato's problem is generally applicable to all our knowledge. The significant point for Polanyi becomes, then, not Plato's "answer" of "remembrance" (the meaning of which he leaves to scholars versed in Platonic thought), but the very posing of the question in this manner along with its consequences for understanding knowledge.

16. *The Tacit Dimension*, p. 22.

17. "The Creative Imagination," *Chemical and Engineering News*, XLIV (April, 1966), 93.

18. This is the sort of description Polanyi often gives concerning the prevailing understanding of the nature of scientific knowledge in his writings. For typical examples, see "From Copernicus to Einstein," *Encounter*, V (September, 1955), 56 and *The Study of Man*, p. 20. Obviously, since Polanyi's intent is to encapsulate the dominant tendency, there is an oversimplification here which does not sufficiently distinguish between a strictly positivistic view (and its variants) and an instrumentalist view, though Polanyi himself usually has in mind positivism. This is quite understandable because Polanyi is not trying to present the merits of the dominant view of science, but to argue for his own "realist" view, sometimes in an openly polemical style. For a more balanced and very clear summary of these varying interpretations, see Ian G. Barbour, *Issues in Science and Religion* (Englewood Cliffs, N.J.: Prentice-Hall, Inc., 1966), pp. 162-171.

19. See Polanyi, "On the Introduction of Science into Moral Subjects," *The Cambridge Journal*, VII (January, 1954), 197 and "From Copernicus to Einstein," 62.

20. Polanyi, "Scientific Beliefs," *Ethics*, LXI (1950), 29.

21. *Science, Faith and Society*, p. 29.

22. *Personal Knowledge*, pp. 160-171.

23. The term is from Thomas S. Kuhn, but it fits in well with Polanyi's understanding of the function of tradition in the scientific community. See Kuhn's *The Structure of Scientific Revolutions* (Chicago: University of Chicago Press, Phoenix books, 1964), especially pp. 46-50 where he argues that paradigms, in addition to explicit rules or canons, guide the process of normal science.

24. "From Copernicus to Einstein," 61.

25. *Science, Faith and Society*, p. 40.

26. These quaint views are discussed by Polanyi in "The Creative Imagination," 86.

27. See the introduction entitled "Background and Prospect" to the 1964 Phoenix book edition of *Science, Faith and Society*, pp. 12-13, where Polanyi points to several philosophers and scientists who all expound views similar to his on the nature of science, though independently and from different perspectives.

28. "The Spirit of the Earth," in *Human Energy* (New York: Harcourt Brace Jovanovich, Inc., 1969), p. 20.

29. Grene, *The Knower and the Known*, p. 14.

30. *Ibid.*, p. 185.

31. *Ibid.*, pp. 190-191.

32. *Ibid.*, p. 239. See also her essay, "The Logic of Biology," in *The Logic of Personal Knowledge* (London: Routledge & Kegan Paul, 1961), especially pp. 201-202, where she analyzes N. Tinbergen's *The Herring Gull's World* which purports to be an "objectivist" account of this species. Yet it is shot through with assertions and observations that go far beyond any merely phenomenal description of these birds (implying by this that it is a much better work). Grene concludes, "in short, Tinbergen, for all his objectivistic faith, gives overwhelmingly the impression of a man who knows not so much the physics of muscle contraction or the chemistry of nuclear proteins, as *sea-gulls*, and that in a personal way that is different from knowing physical or chemical phenomena or even from knowing buttercups and worms."

33. "On the Introduction of Science into Moral Subjects," 195.

34. See *Personal Knowledge*, pp. 369-373 and "Problem Solving," *The British Journal for the Philosophy of Science*, VIII (1957), 90.

35. *The Concept of Mind* (New York: Barnes & Noble, Inc., 1967; original edition 1949), p. 58. It is instructive

to note at this point a recent compilation on this problem from the perspective of the language-analysis school,
entitled *The Philosophy of Mind* (Englewood Cliffs, N.J.:
Prentice-Hall, Inc., 1962). In his introduction to the
volume, the editor, V. C. Chappell, proposed to integrate
the collected articles by viewing them as possible responses to the problem of solipsism, which he regarded as
logically plausible, but somehow faulty since solipsism is
unacceptable. In his development of the solipsistic argument, Chappell continually equates "knowledge" with
"absolute certitude." Chappell's introductory scheme
thus indirectly substantiates Polanyi's contention that
from an objectivist framework "other minds" become problematic.

36. *The Study of Man*, p. 65; "The Structure of Consciousness,"
    p. 216.

37. *Personal Knowledge*, p. 287. For a different perspective
    on this same insight, see Michael Novak's provocative
    study, *The Experience of Nothingness* (New York: Harper
    & Row, Publishers, 1970) wherein he argues that we all
    live within a world structured by some "myth" and can
    only come to this realization at the brink of "nothing-
    ness" when we recognize ourselves as being made by the
    myth we choose and erect. Obviously, this experience
    does not come to all.

38. *Personal Knowledge*, pp. 16-17. Another description of
    this provided by Polanyi states that pseudo-substitution
    "consists in using objectivist terms which are strictly
    speaking nonsensical, as pseudonyms for the mentalistic
    terms they are supposed to eliminate." See "On Body and
    Mind," *New Scholasticism*, XLIII (1969), 204.

39. *Personal Knowledge*, pp. 371-372 and "On Body and Mind,"
    204.

40. "From Copernicus to Einstein," 63.

41. "The Stability of Beliefs," *The British Journal for the
    Philosophy of Science*, III (1952), 217 and 227.

42. "Science and Conscience," *Religion in Life*, XXIII (1953),
    54.

43. *Personal Knowledge*, p. 234.

44. *The Logic of Liberty* (Chicago: University of Chicago
    Press, 1951), pp. 98-99.

45. This term was first used by Polanyi, I believe, in *The
    Logic of Liberty*, p. 106. He had developed the idea ear-
    lier, however, in *Science, Faith and Society* (see especi-
    ally pp. 74-80) where he maintained that a free society
    flourishes by dedicating itself to transcendent ideals
    and that totalitarianism and nihilism were the logical
    outcome of a totally critical stance, unleashing moral
    passions which had no intrinsic value or stability and

which eventually turned on their authors. For Polanyi's
further development of this idea, see the following works
which shall be used in the subsequent explication of this
aspect of his theory: "Science and Conscience," 47-58;
"The Magic of Marxism," *Encounter*, VII (December, 1956),
5-17, later substantially incorporated into *Personal
Knowledge*, pp. 227-232; *Personal Knowledge*, pp. 224-245;
in *Knowing and Being*, "Beyond Nihilism," pp. 3-23, "The
Message of the Hungarian Revolution," pp. 24-39, and "The
Two Cultures," pp. 40-46; "History and Hope: An Analysis
of Our Age," *Virginia Quarterly Review*, XXXVIII (1962),
177-195; "On the Modern Mind," *Encounter*, XXIV (May,
1965), 16-20; and *The Tacit Dimension*, pp. 55-63, 80-87.

46. For a more detailed analysis of this aspect of Polanyi's
thought, see Donald W. Millholland, "Beyond Nihilism:
A Study of the Thought of Albert Camus and Michael
Polanyi" (unpublished Ph.D. dissertation, Duke University, Durham, N.C., 1966).

47. This is the major contention of Marjorie Grene's appraisal of Sartre. In her analysis of *Being and Nothingness* she argues that Sartre remains essentially within
the Cartesian framework of knowledge, even though Sartre
is working out of a pre-reflective cogito. For, while
Sartre recognizes that we must abandon the primacy of
knowledge (in order to avoid the infinite regress of the
idea ideae), he still holds that consciousness of self
alone is non-thetic or precognitive whereas our consciousness of an object is always thetic. This effectively truncates his insight, because Sartre must now
hold that all knowledge (of the world) is explicit and
demands total clarity. Or in Polanyi's terms, Sartre
would allow a tacit recognition of the self (although
this would not be "knowledge" strictly speaking) but
would deny any tacit awareness of the world, thus isolating the cogito within itself. See "Tacit Knowing and
the Pre-reflective Cogito," in *Intellect and Hope*, ed.
by Thomas A. Langford and William H. Poteat (Durham,
N.C.: Duke University Press, 1968), pp. 19-57.

48. Parenthetically this throws light on how Sartre could
assert, in *Critique de la raison dialectique* (Paris:
Editions Gallimard, 1960), pp. 9-10, that a structural
and historical anthropology "finds its place within the
Marxist philosophy. . .because I consider Marxism as the
unsurpassable philosophy of our time and because I hold
the ideology of existence and its 'comprehensive' method
as an enclave within Marxism itself which both engenders
and refuses it at the same time." The first part of
this work, the *Questions de méthode*, was translated into English as *Search for a Method* (New York: Alfred A.
Knopf, Inc., 1963). In her introduction to the trans-
lation, Hazel E. Barnes interprets this work as a way of
understanding how the vision of man propounded earlier
by Sartre could be understood within the world, that is,
as not simply isolated and alone. The similarity of the
dynamics of both existentialism and Marxism as seen by
Polanyi's analysis perhaps clarifies this further.

49. Zdzislaw Najder takes exception to Polanyi's analysis, particularly his description of Marxism as an example of moral inversion, in "'Moral Inversion'--Or Moral Revaluation?" (*Intellect and Hope*, pp. 364-385). Najder correctly points out that Polanyi uses the term "Marxism" in a general sense as the ideology practiced in Communist countries. He takes this as an inadequacy, since he holds that Stalinism, to which Polanyi is often really referring, is a blatant discrepancy between theory and practice (p. 375). Polanyi's contention would assert simply that in fact this is Marxism and Stalin was acting consistently within its framework, even though other Marxists would take another direction. Beyond this, however, he criticizes Polanyi's interpretation of Marxism precisely in the way Polanyi explains that a Marxist would criticize an attack on Marxism! That is, he says Polanyi fails to show the social mechanisms that would validate his interpretation, implying thereby that Polanyi is unscientific (p. 369), and then he shows the moral superiority of Marxism by exposing the flaws of liberal (dare we say bourgeois) nineteenth century Europe and (incorrectly) identifying Polanyi's call for a renewal with a restoration of this past epoch (pp. 380-382). Finally, as the title of the article implies, Najder seems to hold that Marxism is a moral revaluation rather than an inversion. Through the introduction of the notion of a metalanguage of moral philosophy, he wishes to separate moral "passion" from moral "ideas" and then to analyze Marxism as a revaluation--"a shift from one system to another"--thereby allowing investigation according to this scientific language (p. 373). But this is to dichotomize reality, to separate activity from essence or form, something which Najder himself would not otherwise do, at least insofar as he praises Polanyi for pointing out how we cannot escape our commitments (p. 385). In spite of these objections to Najder's basic critique of Polanyi, we wish to say that he does point out some clarifications necessary in order to see the political relevance of Polanyi's thought, particularly the relationship of Polanyi's ontological assumptions to his overall position and the need for precise interpretation of Polanyi because of his penchant for expressing himself in polar and absolute terms (pp. 372-373). We shall not pursue this here, however, for it would carry us far beyond the scope of our study, into concerns of the political scientist.

50. "The Magic of Marxism," 8; *Personal Knowledge*, p. 230.

51. *Personal Knowledge*, p. ix; *The Tacit Dimension*, p. 81.

52. *The Tacit Dimension*, pp. 3 and 60.

53. Ileana Marculescu, "Odyssey of a Humanist," *Center Report*, IV (April, 1971), 6.

54. Colin L. Westerbeck, Jr., "The Confession," *Commonweal*, XCIII (March 5, 1971), 548-549; the italics are in the original.

38

55. This is how Richard Pipes, Associate Director of Harvard's Russian Research Center at the time, regretfully reports the reason for his delay in asserting the explanation Polanyi suggests. See Polanyi's "The Message of the Hungarian Revolution," p. 26.

56. As a result of Polanyi's work in this area, along with the work of others, of course, there has been much progress made in this direction. See, for example, Paul C. Roberts, "Politics and Science," *Ethics*, LXXIX (April, 1969), 235-241, who criticizes earlier inadequate treatments of Polanyi's thought done from the "value-free" perspective.

57. *The Tacit Dimension*, p. 25.

58. "Scientific Beliefs," 33.

59. *Science, Faith and Society*, p. 33.

60. *The Study of Man*, p. 12; the original is italicized.

CHAPTER III

THE HUMAN MODE OF KNOWING

A. The Tacit Component of Human Knowledge

1. The "problem" of knowledge

From at least the time of Newton's great discoveries in physics, man began to see that creative insight consisted in more than simply "looking out there." That what we experience is determined to some extent by the intelligible forms we use to shape our perception was becoming increasingly clear to Western consciousness. The problem for knowledge then is how this is done and what happens to us and to "reality" (insofar as it is known) while we do it. For it is quite conceivable that in our intelligent shaping of our perceptions of reality, we so affect them that these experiences are valid only for describing our mental states, not for telling us what is "really out there."

The confluence of traditional Western conceptions of knowledge and of the demands imposed upon this conception by the new science led, not too surprisingly, to a stalemate. As a result we are left with the inadequacies, exposed in the previous section, of the myth of objectivity confronted by the myth of subjectivity. From the perspective of today we can easily see that the men of the Enlightenment were not so free from the bonds of external tutelage in regard to this core problem of the concept of knowledge as they had supposed. For if this point is considered closely, it becomes apparent that what the intelligentsia of the Enlightenment thought science should be was at odds with what they implicitly knew science to be. The demands of reconciling this solely in terms of explicit criteria led them into a dichotomous and polar position.

To clarify this further let us consider for a moment what science was for Aristotle.[1] Science deals, for him, with the necessary; it is true and certain. We understand, in Aristotle's view, when we know the cause of something and know from this cause that the effect cannot be other than it is. Thus, as a result of its being necessary, our knowledge is metaphysically certain and absolutely true. In the modern sciences, however, the intelligibility sought is contingent. It could very well be other than it is, so it is in need of verification. Certainty in turn gives way to probability and is at best a limiting concept. And due to the ongoing nature of science, truth becomes relativized, if it is retained at all as some sort of a meaningful concept.

But for our purposes, the most important of the notes of Aristotelian science lies in his contention that there is a fundamental distinction between theory and practice. Because science dealt with the necessary and the changeless, all men could do scientifically was a form of contemplation. Science, in other words, totally prescinds from the realm of practical activity. In modern science, however, this is radically changed. Theory describes the realm of practicability. Theory and practice are inextricably interwoven. Science cannot be done without theory as its basis and without this theoretical base there would not be any activity called science.

In effect the modern era has tried to achieve the impossible synthesis of the serenity of detached Aristotelian contemplation in science and of the engaged pursuit into heretofore unexplored realms of reality, endowing them with genuinely novel forms of intelligibility. Within such an assumed framework of viewing knowledge, the disjunction of a neutral objectivity to be played off by an impassioned subjectivity was bound to result. Thus we may say that the problem of knowledge arose in modern times with the recognition of our ability to discover new problems, our practical ability to propose meaningful solutions, and our technological ability to implement these discoveries in effective channels--while at the same time ignoring this tremendous feat on the theoretical level.

In short the problem of knowledge centers on our knowledge of problems. For Polanyi, our knowledge of a good problem constitutes a real advance in knowledge, a genuine discovery in itself.[2] The difficulty in acknowledging our knowledge of problems as paradigm cases of knowing, of course, is paramount in any objectivist scheme, as we have already seen. The reason for eliminating genuine discovery from the knowing process, Polanyi contends, lies in some such rationale as this:

> Since our imagination can roam unhindered by argument and our intuitions cannot be accounted for, neither imagination nor intuition are deemed rational ways of making discoveries. They are excluded from the logic of scientific discovery, which can deal then only with the verification or refutation of ideas after they have turned up as possible contributions to science.[3]

In other words, because a creative and truly innovative discovery cannot be accounted for according to some set of *explicit* canons, it is thereby excluded from the realm of knowledge.

For Polanyi, on the other hand, this difficulty in applying strictly objective and explicit criteria to our recognition of problems means something entirely different. Rather than dismissing problems as significant clues to understanding what it is that we are doing when we know, he suggests that we should admit as an essential element in the knowing process the kind of illuminating groping that describes our recognition of a problem. This is of central importance to Polanyi's theory of knowledge.[4] Its significance can be seen by the curious fact that a problem or a discovery does not exist without a person. "Nothing is a problem or discovery in itself; it can be a problem only if it puzzles and worries somebody and a discovery only if it relieves somebody from the burden of a problem."[5]

Anyone who has ever attempted to "teach" someone knows how difficult is the process of assisting others to wrestle with a problem or comprehend a proposed solution. A major reason for this is that a real discovery is an irreversible process. There are as yet no clearly visible logical steps you may jump back and forth over. Once an insight is attained, however, the problem vanishes. *After* the insight has been achieved or the discovery has been made, explicit forms of logic and reasoning may then be brought forth in an attempt to validate the new solution. But in themselves these arguments may often be weak, inconclusive, inadequate, or even faulty

without thereby invalidating the discovery. We can clearly
exemplify this latter possibility by recalling the cases of
Copernicus and Kepler.[6] Thus the personal judgment of the
discoverer normally has precedence over the reasons he gives
for his discovery.

This does not mean, quite obviously, that there is no
such thing as evidence for or against any so-called discovery.
It simply means, at this stage of our exposition of Polanyi's
theory, that the most important factor in estimating any evidence is the personal appraisal of the knower. Surprisingly
enough, one of the most forceful expressions of this insight
comes from Immanuel Kant. Even the philosopher who tried to
determine the formal rules of pure reason had to admit an unknown factor in every human judgment. He points out that the
faculty of understanding, which is the faculty of rules, is
complemented by the faculty of judgment, which is able to apply
a specific rule in a given case. The faculty of understanding,
accordingly, cannot contain rules for the faculty of judgment
because every time a new instance was to be judged, a new rule
would be needed. Kant then continues:

> This, because it is a new rule, requires a new pre-
> cept for the faculty of judgment, and we thus learn
> that, though the understanding is capable of being
> improved and instructed by means of rules, the
> faculty of judgment is a special talent which can-
> not be taught, but must be practised. This is what
> constitutes our so-called mother wit, the absence
> of which cannot be remedied by any schooling. For
> although the teacher may offer, and as it were
> graft into a narrow understanding, plenty of rules
> borrowed from the experience of others, the faculty
> of using them rightly must belong to the pupil him-
> self, and without that talent no precept that may
> be given is safe from abuse.[7]

Why Kant did not probe more deeply into the significance of the
insight can only be understood by recalling the total fascination of the mainstream of Western thought with the ideal of
explicit knowledge and the separation of this from practical
knowledge. In order to recognize any significance for "our
so-called mother wit," the ideal would have to be altered and
the separation denied.

By accepting our recognition of a problem as the paradigm
case of knowledge, we begin to achieve the transition. We ad-

Implied in this proposal is the recognition that there is no such thing as a totally explicit knowledge. All our knowledge is tacit or based on tacit knowledge. As a result, focal and subsidiary awareness, while they always operate together in the act of knowing, are nevertheless mutually exclusive. (You cannot focus and rely on something at the same time.) And again anytime we are focally aware of something, we are always depending upon some subsidiary awareness.

Our subsidiary awareness may range over many grades of consciousness from subliminal unconscious clues of the processes within our bodies to more or less conscious recognition of particulars functioning as clues. With our subsidiary awareness then we dwell in a whole panorama of realities which we use to focus on distinct aspects. This is how we come to know a problem, in Polanyi's estimation. We do not know, explicitly, what we are looking for, yet we are tacitly able to anticipate what we do not yet understand because of our subsidiary awareness of the particulars which will eventually provide the solution--or prove us wrong.

Within this framework for understanding human knowledge, the personal contribution of the knower means that in the activity of knowing we shape ourselves and create what we are as persons. We do this by incorporating these particulars of our subsidiary awareness into ourselves in order to focus on some feature of that of which we are aware.[11] The acceptance of tacit knowledge and the personal participation of the knower in all acts of knowing has led to the further recognition of *knowing as doing*, affecting the very reality of a person. This is reflected in such statements as, "He is a doctor." This statement means more than the fact that the person identified knows something about the normal functioning of the human body and how to treat certain malfunctions. It also describes the kind of person he is. Therefore besides having implications for understanding the relationship between the various realms of knowledge and the integration of practical and theoretical knowledge as gradations on a continuum, this already indicates a preliminary possible meaning for religious statements: the person who sincerely expresses them has created himself differently from the person who does not.

mit, for example, that a discovery is significant for science (or any endeavor constituting a realm of study) only in the context of a framework or paradigm which cannot be completely set out in explicit, logical terms. The framework, against which the discovery stands out and becomes meaningful, is known only indirectly by studying science, living in a scientific milieu, and letting science become a part of you. "In this respect science is like music or religion which can be recognized only by applying oneself to them."[8] The sharp distinction between theory and practice is thus withdrawn and at the same time a continuity among all forms of knowledge may begin to be appreciated. Similarly, the ideal of total objectivity is being altered, for while "there are rules which give valuable guidance to scientific discovery,. . .they are merely *rules of art*. The application of rules must always rely ultimately on acts not determined by rule."[9] In the final analysis, Polanyi is saying, knowledge is a skill which we can understand most fully not in our ordinary everyday application of it where most of what we are doing goes unnoticed, but in the "boundary situation" where a different framework or a significant challenge to our framework confronts us. "Such confrontations exhibit the essential, if ordinarily submerged structure of all judgment. We have to choose. . .not only which action, but in light of what criteria the choice is to be made."[10]

This then is the "problem" of knowledge as Polanyi has come to see it. His major contribution to contemporary thought consists in a sweeping proposal, first expressed in Chapter Four of *Personal Knowledge*, that we are able to deal with the ambiguity inherent in all acts of knowledge by recognizing two distinct kinds of awareness which work together in every act of knowledge. That which we normally call knowledge, where we explicitly know something, is our *focal* awareness of it. That which we rely on, as a clue or instrument to point to the object of our attention, is our *subsidiary* awareness of these unspecifiable particulars. In a similar manner our knowledge is of two kinds: that which is objectively set out through words or formulae is explicit knowledge, while that which we do not formulate is tacit knowledge.

But this only points to a more crucial facet of Polanyi's theory that must be investigated. How valid is any supposed self-modification due to our participation in the activity of knowing? Or can a theory of knowledge which admits the personal involvement of the knower be justified as more than sheer subjectivism? To explore more fully the meaning of tacit knowing, its relationship to explicit knowledge, and the possibility of validating it will be the concerns of the remainder of this chapter.

2. A preliminary description of tacit knowing

By accepting our knowledge of problems as the paradigm case of knowing, we admit that our knowledge is a skillful performance involving the whole person rather than only some abstract or objective formalization. We are involved in our acts of knowledge because knowing is primarily something we do, not something we have. Knowledge is our chief skill which takes time and practice to acquire and even greater effort to become proficient in some area. Thus in every act of knowledge, including the exact sciences,[12] the personal appraisal of the knower intercedes in the application of a formalization--be it mathematics or the English language--to his experience. This ability to achieve such an integration is, generally speaking, the constituent feature of the tacit dimension of human knowledge.

To begin the description of tacit knowing, then, we shall look at what is involved in skillful performances. A more thoroughgoing analysis of the aspects of tacit knowing would require greater precision than this, but since our concern at this stage is to focus on the personal involvement of the knower in the knowing activity such a discussion will be postponed. As we have indicated above, Polanyi first expressed the fundamental elements of tacit knowing by means of the analogy with skills.[13] Here was a prefiguration of the technical description he later worked out.

Polanyi begins by pointing to the commonly known fact that skills are activities which follow sets of rules not consciously observed by the doer while he is in the process of the performance. This is true not only of obvious skills, such as playing golf or typing, but also of distinctly intellectual activities, such as writing English sentences and doing scientific research. For example, when someone plays golf he is not consciously concerned with the correct "form" for hitting the ball--unless he slices or hooks it. Then he may go back over his swing to try to discover what he did wrong in order to make a mental note of it and to correct it the next time. Similarly when someone writes sentences he is not consciously concerned about the "rules" of grammar and style--unless what was just written sounds wrong or cumbersome. Then he may go over it to try to make the sentence conform to customary usage or flow more gracefully.

In these examples the personal participation of the agent is clear. Yet it is equally clear that there is an element in these skills which is subject to some degree of analysis and is thus, to that extent at least, impersonal insofar as the skill is concerned. Nevertheless such analysis, in terms of the skill, is destructive of the skill while the analysis is being performed. One may, for example, view motion study films of great golfers in order to analyze their form and conceivably one may even write an intricate manual based on this, explaining with a theoretical model of mechanics applied to muscular coordination and illustrating in detail various facets of a proper golf swing. But a student of golf, no matter how well he comprehends, must make the theory real by applying it; no manual can do that. If the student concentrates on one or another aspect of the proper form, he will most likely miss the smooth, rhythmic whole that a properly executed golf swing is and hit poorly. By alternately concentrating on various elements, however, he gradually shifts his focus from the disparate parts to the integral act of "hitting the ball" and proceeds to do so.

While this preceding description may appear to be all too obvious or even trivial, it must not on that account be taken to be irrelevant. The reason is that for Polanyi the analysis of a skill along these lines shows concretely the fundamental structure of all our attempts to relate to reality. In addition to any theoretical framework we may use to aid in our performance of a skill or our understanding of a reality, there is

the further necessary personal ability to achieve or recognize
what the theory abstractly and incompletely sets out--be this
achievement or recognition a skill or "knowledge" as such.   In
other words, all our knowledge encompasses two components--the
explicit and the tacit.

Careful attention must be paid to what Polanyi is saying
here.   He is not simply claiming, as many of his critics are
willing to grant,[14] that in any particular instance of knowing
there are unspecifiable particulars that contribute to our
comprehension of something.   Such a claim could carry with it
the implication that someday, perhaps at present only in the
unforeseeable future, these unspecifiable elements will be
eliminated.   This sort of qualification, probably a carryover
from the modern quest for objectivity, would effectively negate
Polanyi's discovery, for the crucial element in his theory of
knowing is that this dynamic tacit ground permeates *all* our
knowledge as its necessary constituent.

This means, therefore, that the tacit base is always
operable *in principle*, or *of necessity*, in any particular act
of knowledge, even though by shifting our focus what was previously subsidiarily known may now be focally or explicitly
known.   The structure of our acts of knowledge, whereby that
which we focally comprehend by means of a subsidiary reliance
on unspecifiable particulars, can now be clarified by looking
briefly at these four aspects.

a)   The use of tools and frameworks

The tacit root of all our knowledge can be seen by means
of the relationship which always functions between our focal
and subsidiary awareness.   A simple, but clear illustration
offered by Polanyi may be derived from the use of tools.   If
we consider what we are doing while driving a nail with a hammer, we can see that the focus of our attention is absorbed by
the act of driving the nail into the wood.   But certainly we
are aware of more than the head of the hammer striking the
nail.   The effects of using the hammer on our palm and fingers
are just as significant, even though we are aware of them in
quite a different manner.   These feelings are indispensible for
the proper motor control of our arm, and thus for the correct

use of the hammer. The difference is that we rely on these stimuli subsidiarily in order to use the hammer as an instrument to achieve our focal aim.

Because of this dependence of interaction by focal awareness upon subsidiary awareness, it is apparent that these two different kinds of awareness are mutually exclusive. If an agent focuses on a subsidiary element of an act, he will often become confused or make a mistake in terms of the whole activity from which his focal attention was momentarily distracted. This happens whenever we shift our focal attention to particulars of which we had previously been aware subsidiarily. Neophytes in any skill often exemplify this inadvertent shift of attention to a particular, faulting their performance.

That which makes some element of our knowledge subsidiary, then, is not determined solely or even primarily by the fact that it is unspecifiable at the time of the performance of the act. Rather, something becomes subsidiary because of the logical relationship it assumes in the act. If we rely on it in order to focus on something else, it functions subsidiarily in the act. This means, of course, that many things which function subsidiarily may not be entirely specifiable. They may in their turn be known focally, though now by relying subsidiarily on a different set of particulars, including perhaps what was just previously the whole. Often this shifting of our focus from particulars to a whole is the way we learn, as the discussion on the golf swing showed.

By moving on to consider our knowledge of externality and our experience of the parts of our bodies, we can further clarify the functional relationship between subsidiary awareness and focal awareness. We become aware of the myriad processes which are going on in our bodies and which are contributing to our perception of an external object only subsidiarily in terms of the object focally perceived. Similarly our use of tools may now be described as a matter of incorporation, as an effort at making the tools function analogously to the parts of our body on which we subsidiarily rely. When we use a tool skillfully, it is not an external object. During its use it always functions as part of us, the operating persons who subsidiarily rely on it by dwelling in it, just as we dwell in our bodies.

Finally the frameworks of the various kinds of language we use--such as common-sense or everyday speech, scientific formulae, and philosophical and theological discourse--are all known subsidiarily during the actual speaking, formulating, or discoursing. By relying on these frameworks we are able to focus on the many facets of experience they intelligibly open to us. Their presuppositions can only be tacitly assumed for we must dwell in these frameworks, let them become a part of us as we let a tool become a part of us, in order for them to function. All our explicit assertions are then made from within such a framework. Since our explicit utterances rely on these frameworks and can be made only from within some intellectual framework, it follows that the assumptions involved in an actual framework cannot be asserted while we dwell in that framework. They are necessarily inarticulable and can function only tacitly.

b) *Connoisseurship and the recognition of physiognomies*

So far in our analysis of Polanyi's thought we have seen that two different *kinds* of attention, not simply two degrees of attention, are involved in skillful acts of knowledge. We are aware of the same set of particulars in two different ways --focusing on the joint set of particulars by subsidiarily incorporating them into ourselves. This process can now be examined further in terms of perception.

Connoisseurship manifests the same qualities that we have seen in skills and the use of tools. An expert wine-taster or tobacco-judge relies on many subsidiary elements in order to assess just the right combination of particulars. Since it requires a delicately balanced and highly specialized form of perception, connoisseurship can usually be communicated by example alone. The long hours students spend in the laboratory performing relatively trivial exercises under the guidance of more experienced men shows how crucial this master-pupil relationship in the transfer of perceptual skills is even in science. Only when the particular elements which were previously incorporated in some kind of connoisseurship may be easily isolated, standardized, and controlled can the connoisseur be replaced by a machine or a set of rules.

Certain medical diagnoses further illustrate the tacit

reliance on subsidiaries involved in our perception of phenomena. Consider the following story related by Polanyi:

> A few years ago a distinguished psychiatrist demon-
> strated to his students a patient who was having a
> mild fit of some kind. Later the class discussed
> the question whether this had been an epileptic or
> hystero-epileptic seizure. The matter was finally
> decided by the psychiatrist: "Gentlemen," he said,
> "you have seen a true epileptic seizure. I cannot
> tell you how to recognize it; you will learn this
> by more extensive experience."[15]

Due to his experience and training the psychiatrist was able
to recognize the many facets that constitute epilepsy--even
though he knew them only subsidiarily in the total phenomenon
he saw. He recognized the "physiognomy," as Polanyi calls it,
not the isolated particulars. Gradually his students would be
able to achieve this same feat.

The recognition of physiognomy, then, may be a highly
developed skill such as those which abound in the sciences:
in addition to the above illustration, consider the ability to
see something in an X-ray picture or to recognize a leaf as a
particular subspecies. But beyond these special cases, the
ability to recognize a physiognomy is a common occurrence--
when we figure out a jig-saw puzzle, return to a familiar
street in our hometown, or meet a friend. Our ability to recognize objects generally is rooted in our tacit awareness of
particulars which contribute to make the object appear to us
in a familiar--that is, learned--form.

From all of this a further point may now be brought out.
A muscular skill, such as a golf swing, is continuous with the
skill involved in various kinds of connoissuership, which in
turn is continuous with the skills involved in the recognition
of a physiognomy. Underlying all of them is the same pervading structure of a tacit reliance on particulars in order to
focus on a whole. While there is a difference between "knowing
how" and "knowing *that*," the difference is not absolute. It
is, rather, one of degree where the gradual transition between
the extreme poles is hardly noticeable in the complex acts of
knowledge such as our recognition of physiognomies. There is,
then, a continuous gradation in our ability to relate to the
world ranging from our inarticulate and primarily bodily

activities to our highly theoretical and primarily mental activities. That the latter is the case may be grasped by exploring briefly how we attribute meaning to things.

c) Words and meanings

Our ability to relate to reality is accomplished by our giving meaning to it. If something were totally meaningless to us, we would not--even more aptly put, we could not--see it. Not until some object, idea, or aspect of reality can be made meaningful in terms of an intellectual, emotional, or practical framework upon which we rely, can it be present to our focal attention. This is illustrated in the typical theme of Gestalt psychology where an object becomes a tool when it is apprehended in terms of some context. Something will be meaningful for us, then, only if an integration is achieved, an integration demanding a tacit reliance on a set of particulars jointly apprehended as an integral whole.

The words we use are the primary tools, though not the only ones, for accomplishing this. The so-called "transparency" or "open-texture" of language permit us to rely on it subsidiarily in order to focus on the meaning conveyed. Anyone who has struggled to learn a foreign language can appreciate this. At the beginning of this process we must focus on the strange sounds themselves and by relying on an abstract set of grammatical rules and our own native language attempt to *derive* some sort of meaning. Eventually we come to rely on the words and focus instead on the meaning they *convey*. We come to "think" in that language.

This dynamic relationship between focal and subsidiary awareness leading to our grasp of meaning may be further specified by the recognition of two kinds of meaning.[16] The most obvious kind of meaning consists in a simple correspondence of a word to an object: "This is a book." In order to recognize an object, we rely on many perceptual and contextual clues. This first kind of meaning Polanyi terms "denotative" or "representative." Since this type of meaning functions within a context, this context also is recognized as meaningful. Our use of the English language, for example, contains a view of the world which includes the scientific, rational assumptions

derived from Western civilization. Through it we come to see
particular things in reality. Our cultural context, then, may
be said to have an "existential" meaning. Because we rely on
the existential meaning of our intelligent framework, the denotative meaning of a particular assertion is taken to be real.

d) *Commitment and universal standards*

So far in this introductory description of human knowing
we have outlined the basic structural relationship in which
subsidiary awareness always *functions* as a set of elements
upon which we rely in order to achieve the integration of our
focal awareness. And we have seen that by means of these tacit
operations we enable objects to *appear* to us in certain familiar ways. Finally we saw that the *meaning* things have for us is
dependent on the contextual framework we are subsidiarily depending upon at that moment.

All these factors point to the conclusion that our knowledge is a highly personal act. We know *reality* only through
the manifold of its elements which we tacitly take into ourselves in order to focus on something from within that base.
Our explicit knowledge of reality is grounded in a personal
commitment--a commitment which includes our adherence to previous articulations of our heritage while at the same time
contributing our own innovative discoveries as universal standards, thereby clarifying and, in some cases, overturning previously held convictions. The entire continuum of human knowledge, from the realm of muscular activities we rely on in the
use of a tool all the way to our highly symbolic theorems, is
highly personal:

> Like the tool, the sign or the symbol can be con-
> ceived as such only in the eyes of a person who
> *relies on them* to achieve or to signify something.
> *This reliance is a personal commitment which is
> involved in all acts of intelligence by which we
> integrate some things subsidiarily to the centre
> of our focal attention.* Every act of personal
> assimilation by which we make a thing form an ex-
> tension of ourselves through our subsidiary aware-
> ness of it, is a commitment to ourselves, a manner
> of disposing ourselves.[17]

Our knowledge accordingly has the effect of disposing ourselves toward some purpose. Through the tacit incorporation of

various elements helpful for relating ourselves in any particular situation we set in motion a heuristic effort. We make
ourselves when we understand reality. This effort, however, is
not totally dynamic or absolutely creative on our part. Whenever we come to know something there is also an element of pas-
sivity to be taken into account: we do not make reality, we
submit to it. In all our knowledge therefore there is present
a sense of obligation toward the truth. No matter how creative
our own insights must be in order to attain any truth, we can
express it only by relying on self-set standards which strive
to be universal.

This intricate network of relationships, within which the
knower already encounters and is shaped by reality before he
proposes his articulate representation of it, saves personal
knowledge from being merely subjective. Because we extend ourselves through our subsidiary awareness of particulars which
constitute a whole, we necessarily participate in shaping all
our knowledge while remaining in the same instant responsible
by asserting it with universal intent.

3. The dimensions of tacit knowing

Now that Polanyi's basic insight, along with a preliminary
description of its chief facets, has been exposed, we shall attempt to consolidate and expand the significance of his theory
of personal knowledge. It would obviously be a practical impossibility to discuss the entire range of our tacit powers,
especially to document the varied types of studies which contributed to Polanyi's analysis. For the purposes of this inquiry, then, we shall try to probe, in a selective fashion, the
importance of the inarticulate foundation of our knowledge for
all our articulate and heuristic endeavors.[18] But beyond this
narrow purpose of practicality, the directions charted here
will be guided by the further criterion of introducing in an
anticipatory manner elements that will later be developed more
thoroughly in our argument.

Polanyi's theory of personal knowledge adapts the traditional epistemological axiom that all knowledge comes through
the senses, by modifying it slightly to say that all thought
has a bodily basis. This implies that all articulations by man

are dependent on inarticulate powers or faculties. There are, as Polanyi would put it, things that we know but cannot speak of. If all our articulate knowledge, then, is dependent on such an inarticulate base, the accreditation of our utterances as true involves the whole of this skillful act--including the tacit domain. Everything we assert as true is thus dependent --in addition to other factors--on personal criteria which we cannot formally define. Since the inarticulate realm must ultimately prove to be decisive in our judgments, articulations of what we deem to be true are always incomplete. Consequently the ideal of objectivity conceived as impersonal detachment will have to be revised in order to account for this personal involvement in all human expressions of truth.

To describe the dimensions of tacit knowing we shall begin at the most rudimentary level of human intelligence: that which lies beyond the realm of language and which we share with animals. By recalling various types of animal learning we shall have at our disposal a prototype of the processes which take place in human knowing at this level.

Experimental psychologists have analyzed animal behavior: when such behavior goes beyond instinctive reaction we have an instance of learning. The results of these studies may be categorized in the following three ways. First are examples of trick learning. These are basically forms of motor learning where the animal contrives a skillful action. Next are cases of sign learning which, in addition to the motility involved, are dependent on perception. Here the animal reorganizes his observational field in order to relate a sign to an event. Finally instances have been discovered of animals achieving what can only be described as a type of latent learning in which the animal possesses a simple non-verbal understanding of a situation. In this case a very primitive form of logical behavior may be observed in the animal in that alternative choices are made in behavior which are not simply random. In addition to this sort of research with animal behavior, it might be noted here that much of the experimental work done with infants and children by Piaget confirms the operation of inarticulate intelligence which grounds all human articulation.

One of the significant results that Polanyi has derived from these studies is the recognition of the irreversibility of the learning process in contrast to the reversibility possible in the display of what is learned. The initial acts of contriving a trick, perceiving a sign, and the gradually building grasp of a situation or the sudden flash of insight into it are all heuristic in character and thus irreversible, whereas the repetition of a trick, the continued response to a sign, and the normal solving of problems are routine in character and thus reversible. Already at this level of existence we are forced to acknowledge two kinds of inarticulate intelligence: one operating heuristically by effecting innovations in its ability to relate to the environment, the other operating from within a set pattern or framework to consolidate its relationship to the environment.

All of these basic types of learning are to be found in man, though at a more highly developed level. The transition in man from a form of latent, inarticulate learning to its articulate counterpart consists in discovering, recognizing, and understanding that the various systems of coherences and logic are the formal expressions of the operational rules which function implicitly in these rudimentary forms of intelligence. Man's vast superiority over animals is due to this greatly increased range of experience and consequent potential for more significant heuristic activity which becomes open to him as a result of his articulate framework.

At this point it will perhaps be helpful to clarify the relationship between inarticulate or tacit knowledge and articulate or explicit knowledge by examining how they both operate in relation to the same subject.[19] If we compare a man's ability to find his way through some unknown and unmarked territory with a rat's ability in running a maze, we would find that there is no immediate inherent superiority in the man—unless he had a map to guide himself. While the rat, by means of trial and error, may eventually develop an inarticulate grasp of the proper route, the man will be able not only to duplicate this feat but also to draw up an explicit map. And if a man had such a map, he would have the great advantage of being able to travel through unfamiliar territory rather easily.

This advantage, however, brings with it the equally disadvantageous possibility of being incorrect. Even though this risk is now there, the ability to reflect critically on the map is also present. This is not the case with inarticulate knowledge: the only way to test an inarticulate grasp of a terrain is by action, by trying this way and that. Inarticulate intelligence can only plod from one viewpoint to another. As opposed to articulate intelligence, it is a-critical.

Clearly, then, it is man's capacity for speech and critical reflection which greatly enhances his tacit powers. Our ability for understanding through the insightful reorganization of our experience does not stop at the immediate threshold of our inarticulate sensory experience. Because animal intelligence remains on the inarticulate level, only one of the possibilities for learning discussed above is available to it at any particular instance. By extending our powers of contriving and observing with a set of symbols--for example, our language --we correspondingly expand our interpretive powers by means of our ability to integrate all three types of learning.

Even so, the symbols we contrive to aid us in our observations are effective only to the extent to which they aid our inarticulate powers to interpret and understand. No matter how sophisticated our symbolic representations become, they are able to function only within the spectrum of inarticulate intelligence we share with animals. Thus Polanyi's explanation of the human mode of knowing recognizes the importance of our articulate constructions and the critical control they provide while at the same time acknowledging the dimensions of tacit knowing which sustain them. "Our whole articulate equipment," he asserts, "turns out to be merely a tool-box, a supremely effective instrument for deploying our inarticulate faculties. And we need not hesitate then to conclude that the tacit personal coefficient of knowledge predominantes also in the domain of explicit knowledge and represents therefore at all levels man's ultimate faculty for acquiring and holding knowledge."[20]

In our ordinary everyday experience, then, we commonly acknowledge instances of knowledge which are unspoken and recognize the fact that many of our insights are at first grasped pre-verbally and need further reflection before they may be expressed conceptually. Polanyi contends that this has long been accepted in philosophical analysis, even though our modern cultural history, with its stress on complete objectivity and detached scientific analysis, tries to deny or at least ignores this dimension by dismissing it as psychological.[21] The preceding discussion was thus a necessary digression in order to emphasize the significance and importance of the personal affirmation of the knower in all acts of knowledge. In tracing the origins of our ability for articulate expression, we encounter the rudimentary forms of learning by which all animal life attempts to relate to its environment. This included man who is able to extend and heighten these tacit powers by his explicit symbols which in their turn are constantly relying on their tacit ground.

With the recognition of the inarticulate basis of our formal expression of thought, we have not only proposed a logical structure for understanding how we hold our ordinary perceptions of reality, but, even more important, for understanding how we hold our loftiest achievements. Through our tacit reliance on our varied articulate frameworks we not only experience reality in a more comprehensive fashion, we also are empowered to experience ever more fully. The tacit grounding and probing which constantly accompany our ordinary use of intellectual frameworks enable us to go beyond these frameworks by means of the intimations of yet undisclosed realities implicit in them. Our tacit powers, in short, both sustain our present articulations and the experience of reality they represent and enable us to discover new modes of articulation by opening to our awareness new aspects of reality.

The fascination and wonder, of which we become aware through our reliance on articulate frameworks, lead man far beyond the narrow range of experience open to animal intelligence. Through these frameworks our tacit powers are expanded to include a whole new range of possible inarticulate responses which are nonetheless still intelligent: these experiences are, in Polanyi's terms, "intellectual passions." Through them we accredit the truth and beauty in a scientific theory, a symphony, a great philosophical insight, or a religious vision.

By attempting to understand some of the elements of the complex process of scientific or mathematical discovery, we hope to provide an illustration to clarify this.

First of all the difference between systematic and heuristic problem solving should be kept in mind. Systematic problem solving is the routine, deliberate activity of consolidating and strengthening an insight already achieved. Because it operates from within a stable context, its processes are predominantly formal and reversible. The heuristic process of problem solving, on the other hand, is irreversible. No explicit rules can account for it beforehand and once achieved it alters the whole perspective of the investigation. Generally it proceeds by an alternative passage through active and passive stages, that is explicit and tacit stages, until the final burst of insight and resolution. It is this second type of discovery with which we are primarily concerned.

Secondly, any proposed discovery can claim significance only within some system or paradigm currently held in science. Since the paradigm itself cannot be expressed in formalized terms, it can be grasped only through the study of science leading to the tacit appropriation and acceptance of the unformalizable premises which sustain the paradigm. Only through this tacit adherence to the framework of science can there be a criterion which could supply the impulse toward discovery and to which the discovery, once achieved, could be referred for judgment.[22]

Thirdly, the frame of reference within which we are analyzing the elements of discovery does not even allow the logical conundrum, which we had seen expressed in Plato's *Meno*, to arise. The activity of looking for the unknown is made intelligible through the recognition and acceptance of our tacit powers. In looking for the unknown, we attempt to apprehend the known data in varied subsidiary ways in order to allow the data to act as guides in shaping our focal awareness to form a conception of a solution.[23]

Finally we are able to understand how the heuristic activity progresses and terminates. Because the inquirer is looking for something of which he has at present only an intimation, he is able to be guided by the degree of coherence his focal attention is providing. That is, if a proposed hypothesis clouds his understanding of the relationship between the data he is subsidiarily attempting to reintegrate, he discards or at least modifies it. If, on the other hand, an alternative hypothesis begins to allow some semblance of coherence to appear in the subsidiarily held data, he pursues it. Eventually the disquietude which perhaps initially provoked the search is resolved with the attainment of the insight which allows the subsidiarily known data to assume a new focal coherence. From this point on the standards implied in the insight are ours; we are committed to them and bring them to bear on all our experience: we have successfully achieved a heuristic leap into the unknown.[24]

Polanyi has expressed the crucial points of the present discussion in a succinct passage about mathematical discovery worth quoting in full:

> The manner in which the mathematician works his way towards discovery by shifting his confidence from intuition to computation and back again from computation to intuition, while never releasing his hold on either of the two, represents in miniature the whole range of operations by which articulation disciplines and expands the reasoning powers of man. This alternation is asymmetrical, for a formal step can be valid only by virtue of our tacit confirmation of it. Moreover, a symbolic formalism is itself but an embodiment of our antecedent unformalised powers; it is an instrument skillfully contrived by our inarticulate selves for the purpose of relying on it as our external guide. The interpretation of primitive terms and axioms is predominately inarticulate and so is the process of their expansion and re-interpretation, which underlies the progress of mathematics. A formal proof proves nothing until it induces the tacit conviction that it is binding. Thus the alternation between the intuitive and the formal depends on tacit affirmations both at the beginning and at the end of each chain of formal reasoning.[25]

Even in such a sphere of highly formal reasoning, the inarticulate demands of the elegance or beauty of a theory are necessarily included in the acceptance and recognition of a discovery.

So far we have tried to clarify how the scope of our inarticulate faculties ranges from their operation in simple perceptual learning to their grounding our highly sophisticated intellectual frameworks and the intellectual passions which provoke, foster, and accredit heuristic discoveries. While the efforts of the knower in shaping his experience are perhaps of paramount importance in these extreme cases, Polanyi's contention is that our tacit powers operate just as thoroughly in the vast bulk of the knowledge which forms the everyday experience of our lives. This may be indicated briefly by considering our knowledge of "facts." What we generally will accredit as a fact is dependent upon our tacit recognition of the way we establish facts. This means that after first accepting certain things as facts (perhaps because of some regular occurrence tacitly experienced and then formally expressed), we may then deduce some rationale to explain this (by means of the method of experimental verification and control, we seek out those phenomena amenable to it and call them scientific facts). But this rationale will always be dependent on our antecedent, tacit accreditation of certain things as facts.[26]

The structure which we saw in discovery is thus operating in our ordinary traffic with daily life. Our intellectual passions are constantly on the alert to recognize new facts and reinterpret old ones. We do this by dwelling in the premisses of authentic instances of mental achievements. Some men are content with this limited form of achievement. Some others do more by striving to consolidate what had been achieved in previous breakthroughs.

Still, there are a very few who are unwilling to remain within the framework which guided them to their maturity. Because of their heightened intellectual passions these men constantly press the frontiers of their conceptual frameworks to break out into new levels of experience and eventually articulation. This is the height of our intellectual passions and the meaning of discovery on all levels. Such breaking out is also of supreme significance for the religious life.

4. The societal characteristics of tacit knowing

So far our analysis of human knowing has tried to show the importance of the personal involvement of the knower in the shaping of his knowledge and exploring the scope of its operations in upholding all our knowledge. A crucial element in this analysis was the recognition that our acceptance of articulate systems was a personal act which we appropriated to ourselves with the conviction that it adequately expanded and developed our tacit powers. Implied in this analysis, then, is the further recognition that the tacit acceptance of an articulate framework has social ramifications. The reason for this, quite obviously, is that articulate frameworks continue to exist only through the support afforded them by a society. The society must accept the values affirmed in the frameworks and the intellectual passions which ground them. Through the common acceptance, sharing, and cultivation of these intellectual passions, the cultural life of a society is realized. Our aim here is to introduce some of these societal characteristics of human knowing from the vantage point of Polanyi's theory.

To begin with, a tacit sharing of knowing underlies all our efforts at communication.[27] This is clearly the case in pre-articulate sharing of experiences, such as the mutual joy of the simple presence of a beloved. The sympathy evoked at the sight of another person in pain is a result of a common tacit bond. And our ability to learn to speak is a further instance. By tacitly accepting the authority of a parent or instructor, a child or student expands his tacit skills by means of the articulate framework conveyed through the language. Articulate communications occur only when the persons involved tacitly accept a similar set of assumptions.

What is true of interpersonal communication is just as true of cultural life in general. The individuals are informed by the culture they inherit, and through their tacit reliance on it transmit it to their offspring modified and developed-- hopefully for the better. This process of being informed necessitates that the individual submit himself to the values sustained by the culture and act in accordance with its standards. It assumes that the individual places his trust in his cultural leaders and that what is now taken on authority will, once mastered and understood, be found meaningful and intellectually satisfying.

The acceptance of a cultural framework thus operates in much the same way as the recognition of a problem. In the latter case our heuristic intimations of a new reality are

activated by our tacit awareness of the particulars on which
we are beginning to rely in order to strain our imagination for
an eventual focal and explicit coherence leading to insight and
discovery. So, too, a novice in the cultural life of a society
tacitly relies on the premises, standards, values, and options
implicit in that culture in order to make them a part of himself and by so doing to view reality from its vantage point.
The major difference lies in the fact that the discoverer is
guided primarily by his personal judgments, while the learner
must primarily place his trust in others. In both cases, however, the discovery and the acculturation are self-modifying
processes which are irreversible and for the most part a-
critical. Of course, once a person has assimilated a cultural
framework sufficiently well, he can often justify himself,
though never completely. The authority of respected leaders
and the general premises commonly and tacitly agreed upon are
always concomitants of any cultural self-accreditation on the
part of an individual member of the society.

While such submission to cultural authorities is a necessary condition for us to acquire its tools as aids in our mental development, it is not on that account a complete and total
determinant of what we are as persons. Every encounter with
authority qualifies it. Even complete dedication to some element of a culture necessitates that the person dedicate himself
in a way he thinks is most appropriate. By identifying himself
with such an element of his culture in *this* way (as opposed to
some other way), the person affects what it is. Inversely,
dissent from a cultural tradition, no matter how radical its
claims, must involve some elements of acceptance of the tacit
communal consensus. No revolution can completely negate preceding cultural forms. Revolutions in a culture occur when
premises, which previously had served as tacit communal bonds,
become questionable. This is possible, and even likely, if
the original premises were fruitful enough to lead a significant number of people beyond the frame of reference circumscribed by these premises. In such instances the cultural
avant-garde assumes a new set of tacitly held premises and by
means of this is able to uncover and analyze some of their
previous assumptions. Because it indirectly forms its present

cultural basis in light of and in response to previously held
common assumptions, the new cultural expression is never completely dichotomous. And since they no longer share completely
the same tacit frame of reference, communication between the
old and the new is difficult and strained, but because the new
grew from the old it still is not precluded. The authority of
the old, lest it become reactionary and despotic as it becomes
more and more unconvincing, must move ahead to adopt the tacit
bonds of the new or be replaced.

Clearly every utterance one makes--whether it be of the
weather, the world series, the stock market, the lunar land-
ings, women's lib, the categorical imperative, or the command-
ment of love--can only be made in reference to a tacitly held
consensus. As individuals in a society we establish a vast
interconnected network of commonly shared premisses. Through
them we support collectively the institutional channels of culture, foster a communal identity, implement an economic system,
and regulate the powers of the society. Every time we shape
ourselves by a new insight or discovery we correspondingly affect this consensus.

In order to examine concretely some of the processes involved in the societal characteristics of human knowing, we
shall now turn to their manifestations in the workings of science. We shall be using, in effect, the structural dynamics of
the scientific community as a paradigm for the functioning of
society in general.[28] This procedure is valid, according to
Polanyi, because science exists and can continue to exist only
through a community of like-minded men who uphold a common tradition, are subject to the authority embodied in that tradition, and strive for similar goals implied in the tradition.
Science functions, in short, by means of a structure similar
to any other cultural expression in which complex creative activities are carried on beyond the lifetime of individuals who
constitute it.[29]

There are many today who might be troubled by this ascrip-
tion of an "authority" controlling the practice of science,
probably because of the popular view of science as founded on
a rejection of authority for the sake of the free pursuit of
the individual scientist. There is, of course, a certain

validity to this view. The authority of Aristotle, Ptolemy,
Galen, and the Bible as interpreted by most Christian leaders
during the Renaissance and Reformation were all rejected in the
formative years of modern science. But the point to note is
that they were rejected in order to establish the authority intrinsic to science itself. Today the authority of science is
almost unchallenged by such extrinsic authority, and the direction taken by science is controlled primarily by the values
upheld by scientists themselves.[30]

The agent of this internal authority for science is scientific opinion. Again this assertion must be taken in the proper
manner, because "a community of scientists in which each would
act only with an eye to please scientific opinion would find no
scientific opinion to please."[31] Furthermore, there is no scientist who grasps the whole that constitutes the scientific
enterprise today. Therefore there is no one scientist who controls scientific opinion as such. Rather, each scientist, by
applying himself rigorously to the values and standards inherent in his work and by judging those in his area of speciali-
zation and those in neighboring areas by these same criteria,
forms, in conjunction with every other scientist, a network
which upholds itself and wards off challenges from outside.[32]
The opinion thus formed is carried on by the tradition embodied
in living scientists who constitute a community with its own
structures of authority enforced through the control of access
to publication in periodicals, of publishing text-books, of ap-
pointments to prestigious positions, and of the general recognition granted to members deemed exceptionally creative.[33]

More specifically we may say that scientific opinion functions and is established according to the principle of mutual
control.[34] Scientists watch over each other by means of chains
of overlapping neighborhoods. Provided the standards of scientific plausibility are equally applied by scientists at each
nexus of the scientific community, a mediated consensus is established whereby all scientists mutually respect each other's
conclusions and support them against any non-scientific challenge. In this way each scientist indirectly controls--and
is, of course, controlled by--the standards of science and
comes to trust findings in branches only distantly related to

his own.

This tension of personal heuristic passions seeking new insight, but always in the context of a presuppositional framework controlled by mutual consent, also accounts for the amazing growth of science. By relying on the currently held framework of the scientific community as a guide to his grasp of reality, the scientist pursues presently unknown possibilities suggested by the existing fund of knowledge. Each step is guided both by his reliance on the tacit premises of the scientific community and his own personal dedication to the as yet elusive reality he is pursuing by means of it.

At rare junctures in the history of science, a scientist's discovery may be so creative as to call for a new presuppositional framework, altering the very meaning of the complex of facts, terms, methods, and problems implied in the old one and demanding a shift in focus or a new perceptual stance which itself goes beyond empirical verification. In short, the dynamics of the scientific community may lead to revolutionary consequences by reshaping the tacit grounds of the community. In order to appreciate this new framework, his fellow scientists must adopt his stance, for it cannot be properly understood from within the old perspective. Through this process of exploring the implications of a current framework and occasionally breaking through to a new framework by means of a reliance on the existing body of knowledge, science maintains its continuity in spite of promoting revolutionary change.[35]

By using the example of science we have seen that persons accept a set of premises embodied in a tradition in order to relate to their fellows and to endow their experience of reality with meaning. Furthermore these premises are not derived by any explicit process from the data of experience, nor can they be verified by any formal set of criteria. They are logically anterior to explicit mental procedures in that they form our idiom of beliefs.[36] Because of this their application relies continually on our personal judgment.

Before we conclude our discussion of the societal characteristics of human knowledge, then, we shall examine the dynamics of our intellectual frameworks insofar as they provide a stable basis for the operation of the idiom of beliefs by means of which we interpret our experience.[37]

As a result of the efforts of cultural anthropologists, it has been brought to our attention that primitive people hold, by means of their linguistic and cultural premises, systems of belief quite different from our own. Anthropologists have further shown that these systems of belief exhibit remarkable resiliancy when confronted by a (Western) scientific challenge. While operating from within the world view circumscribed by their idiom, a member of one of these tribes can consistently maintain his position in the face of objections drawn from outside that idiom.

This in turn has led many Westerners to reflect on their own conceptual frameworks as perhaps sharing in similar characteristics. In some quarters, this has had shattering effects. For while we are willing to recognize that "primitive" peoples have quite limited presuppositional frameworks and thus have difficulty even seeing "facts" (from our perspective, that is) because they are not contained in their idiom of thinking, it is quite another matter for us to admit that our "objective" view of reality also unfolds through our reliance on our own idiom of belief.

But this is precisely the case. All our intelligent apprehensions of reality are relative to the framework on which they rely.[38] Nevertheless these frameworks are endowed with characteristics which provide a form of stability. Consequently any contemporary Western interpretive framework--be it Freudianism, Marxism, Barthianism, or, for that matter, "Polanyianism"--tends to be seen as all-embracing by its adherents. The reason for this is that while we rely on any particular idiom of belief, everything we ask will be formulated in terms of it. This obviously tends to confirm the world view implicit in it. It also underscores the difficulty of questioning an assumption contained within a world view from within the idiom espousing that world view. Normally we must accept a new idiom of thought before we will even have at our disposal a language which will allow us to question our former premisses.

In order to complete our appraisal of the societal characteristics of tacit knowing, therefore, we shall attempt to describe the dynamic processes which endow idioms of belief with this stability. These may be conveniently categorized as having characteristics which are circular, which employ epicyclic reserve, and which suppress nucleation of new ideas.

Through the circularity of systems of belief, objections to its implicit world view can be met one by one. The doubt raised by one item is dispelled by reliance on past successful applications of the framework. This has the effect of strengthening the premises which were questioned. And when several people interact from within the same idiom of belief, their mutual agreement on the interpretation of a given experience further confirms their mental set.

By means of the epicyclic reserve of an interpretive system, an automatic expansion of the circle is provided to account for almost any conceivable eventuality. These secondary elaborations keep in supply a subsidiary reserve which is necessary for any major idiom of beliefs to survive the challenge of data not immediately accounted for by the main structure of the system.

Finally the principle of suppressed nucleation prevents the germination of any rival concepts by not allowing them any ground in which to take root. By not allowing a possibly meaningful concept of some challenging evidence to operate within the idiom, any such evidence that might eventually lend credence in favor of that concept will simply not be seen or will be disregarded as meaningless and absurd. When working in complementary fashion these three factors can account for the comprehensiveness of a system of beliefs, which we may recognize without thereby implying any validity for the system.

The system of naturalistic beliefs which forms the idiom of scientific thinking is supported by this same dynamic logical structure. A discrepancy between a particular scientific notion and some item of experience will be explained by an appeal to other scientific ideas. The use of the conception of "anomaly" and the deployment of "provisional hypotheses" within a system provide a ready reserve of epicyclic elaborations to sustain the system. And complementing this, science will deny, or dismiss as being of no scientific interest, a vast range of experience which appears vital to other perspectives. One need only recall reductivist accounts of biology or behaviorist interpretations of human consciousness to appreciate this.

This discussion of the societal characteristics of human knowledge leads us to conclude that the comprehensiveness and coherence of a system of beliefs are criteria of its stability more than of its truth. Clearly, a system which is comprehensive and coherent may just as easily stabilize a false view of the universe, and it needs in any case the further acceptance by a group of adherents in order to foster the additional claim to truth. But such an acceptance can only be analyzed from within a perspective, that is, it cannot be analyzed from some privileged "neutral" or "objective" standpoint.

Insofar as this analysis of the societal characteristics of the human mode of knowing shows that an articulate framework cannot be established objectively, it seems as though we may have led ourselves into an intolerable position. We have argued that man must exercise his personal responsibility in upholding all that he knows by tacitly shaping his experience. Yet he can do this only by submission to some conceptual framework whose idiom of belief he accepts and shares and from which his thought unfolds. But if, as we have seen, all such expressions of idioms can meet challenges from outside on its own terms, is there any basis for judging what is really the case? By what criteria and standards may we make such judgments? "On what grounds can we change our grounds? We are faced with the existentialist dilemma: how values of our own choosing can have authority over us who decreed them."[39] Is man condemned to choose between complete subjectivism and bad faith?

The broad outlines of a "solution" begin to emerge as we recognize that even these questions are of our own making and derive from our cultural heritage. Ultimately, then, the final criterion is to be found in our personal judgment. It is, therefore, a criterion in constant growth, development, and expansion which seeks ever more adequate ways of appropriating --and, speaking religiously, of being appropriated by--the mystery of reality. That this cognitive dynamism inherent in man is sufficient for justifying our knowledge is the next subject for our attention.

B. The Validation of Human Knowing

   1. The meaning of validation

   The *ultimate* criterion for establishing the validity of
any intellectual endeavor is the personal affirmation of the
knower.   The stress on "ultimate" is deliberate and important.
When it is a question of validating an articulate framework
with its implicit world view, there are no formal criteria for
establishing some sort of absolute certainty because the application of such criteria necessitates the prior involvement of
the knower in accepting them.[40] Nevertheless people do acknowledge some things to be true.   They do so even though they may
later realize that they were mistaken.   They do so even when
they cannot completely express to themselves their reasons and,
perhaps more frequently, when they cannot express their reasons sufficiently well enough to convince others of their view.
But if we are to avoid falling into complete subjectivism and
relativism, we must be able to explore this process by which a
knower in fact comes to accept something as true.

   The proposal offered by Polanyi to attempt to account in
a meaningful way for this radical foundation of human knowledge
in personal affirmation has already been implicitly introduced.
It consists in analyzing our informal, pre-articulate powers
of thought which underlie and sustain all our explicit canons
of reasoning.   Polanyi's proposal, thus, does not abrogate
logic; it seeks to establish the various modes of logic by
examining the dynamic structure of the entire range of the
knowing process.   This is an ambitious and extremely hazardous
undertaking which is even rejected as impossible or invalid in
some circles.[41] It is Polanyi's contention, however, that only
by means of such a foundational undertaking will man once again
be able to understand and sustain the many dimensions beyond
that of the pragmatic one which constitute and affect his life.

   It order to probe the validity of Polanyi's proposal for
understanding the human mode of knowing, it is necessary to
recall the subtleties involved in any sort of justification of
a claim and to consider the kind of endeavor we are undertaking.   By keeping these factors in mind we may hopefully avoid
unfounded expectations and clarify the requirements of the task

before us.

The demonstration of a proof is not a completely unambiguous activity, no matter how formal are the procedures which may be said to constitute it. A vast array of prior insights and a cumulation of antecedent commitments must accompany and sustain any such demonstration in order that the proof achieve its aim. A discussion of these elements by Polanyi is instructive:

> The mere handling of symbols according to the rules of formal proof constitutes a proof only to the extent to which we accredit these operations in advance with the power of carrying conviction. But "proof" (as I think Ryle would say) is a success-word. The success in this case lies in the capacity of the "proof" to convince us (and to convince us also that others ought to share our conviction) that an implication has been demonstrated. No handling of symbols to which we refuse to award this success can be said to be a proof, no matter what pre-established rules it is said to conform to. And again the award of this success is a process which is not formalised.42

The unformalized tacit powers which we bring to bear upon all our experience are thus crucial for the validity of any proof within a formal discipline. The operation of these tacit powers, moreover, is precisely what we are attempting to analyze and justify. As a result, our attempt at justifying Polanyi's theory will not constitute what is normally meant by a formal proof, since the object of our analysis is precisely that which renders a formal proof personally compelling.

This qualification likewise holds in the realm of empirical verification. Because of the cultural prestige afforded science in the modern era, we are tempted to judge all our mental activities according to the criteria which science is assumed to fulfill. But the history of science is rife with examples where what constitutes a verification of a hypothesis for one scientist is inconsequential, meaningless, or simply incorrect to another. Clearly, the personal judgment of the scientist exercises a formidable role in the process of verification.

This is, of course, implicitly recognized in science by the admission that scientific verification yields probability, not certainty. For to recognize that empirical assertions are not absolutely clear and certain in and of themselves is to include the kind of contingency in scientific knowing that pervades every human judgment. Thus a statement affirmed as probable necessitates a personal judgment just as if affirmed as certain.[43] The process of verification, then, supplies clues and hints which the scientist must accept as compelling even though the risk of error is present and precludes absolute certainty.

So, too, the possibility of falsifying a scientific claim, which would assure its empirical character, requires the personal adjudication of a scientist for its application. It is quite correct, logically speaking, that an empirical generalization is not strictly verifiable, though a falsification of it strictly refutes the generalization. Nevertheless the procedure of falsification is itself not formally determined. While it is, again, correct that one exception logically contradicts a generalization, it is not correct that an apparent contradiction automatically overthrows the generalization. In order for this to occur we must first decide whether the exception is a real contradiction and, if we so decide, then whether it is significant enough to overturn the generalization or only of secondary importance to be set aside temporarily, perhaps as an anomaly.[44]

These brief reflections on some of the procedures we normally acknowledge to be explicit ways of justifying various elements of our knowledge serve to illustrate the complexity of what we take for granted in our reliance upon them. One may see the compelling force of the meaning of the pythagorean theorem in its algebraic or geometric forms of proof, but it is always *some person* who does so. How does he do this? And why? This is the critical problem with which Polanyi's theory attempts to grapple, for it is his contention that this personal coefficient pervades and sustains all human knowing, including the formal procedures we have just described. By examining our cognitional activity at work in such crucial areas we shall then have a better understanding of how it normally functions in our ordinary knowledge.

The consequences of this recognition is that our attempts to demonstrate the validity of the theory of personal knowledge must of necessity share in the complexity inherent in the general question of how we come to discover and accept anything as true. Any objection that there must be some "impersonal" or formal criteria by which to judge Polanyi's theory fails to grasp the kind of problem at issue and the kind of inquiry required to deal with it. Since we are concerned with how we accept such criteria, the theory of personal knowledge can only be found plausible on the very grounds which it exposes for the validity of our knowledge in general. In presenting Polanyi's theory we shall propose a way by which we may accept the personal basis of all knowing; and this effort, if successful, shall turn out to be the justification of personal knowledge itself.

The task before us may perhaps be brought into sharper focus by recalling some of the elements involved in our reliance on articulate frameworks. Whenever a disagreement concerning the meaning of a range of our experience occurs, the resultant controversy can often be settled in a methodical and orderly manner--provided the discussion takes place within the same branch of knowledge and the discussants share a common set of presuppositions. If, however, the conflict arises from the encounter between two opposing frameworks, the outcome will not be decided simply by an appeal to the methods of justification within one or the other position. The less the conflicting opinions have in common, the more the discussion will take on the character of an attempt at conversion where one party tries to show, in general terms which the other party might understand, its own supposed greater rationality or comprehensiveness for understanding the experience in question. The net result, if one party is successful, is that one of the participants will gradually begin to appreciate the other perspective, accept its tacit grounds, and experience a richer mental satisfaction in beholding the same data of experience within the context of this new-found meaning.[45] A process of this sort must take place if the claims of personal knowledge are to be justified.

For these reasons, Polanyi prefers to speak of the *validation* of a system of thought.[46] Certainly within a highly formal system of knowledge, a proof is a meaningful and necessary operation though its validity is dependent upon the prior acceptance, and thus validation, of the system. And similarly because natural science intends to interpret a limited range of human experience in terms of its quantifiable properties, it is quite proper to speak of verification in science once the naturalistic view of the universe is apprehended meaningfully. This is not so, however, of the arts in general and religion in particular. Even though these frameworks of thought do attempt to interpret the meaning of our experience, their dependence on experience is not so readily quantifiable.

Validation thus describes the process by which we come to appreciate and hold a theoretical framework as a meaningful instrument for interpreting our experiences which have a bearing on reality. The more profound the experience, the greater will be our reliance on criteria of internal mental satisfaction and the less on external criteria.[47]

The theory of personal knowledge may now be seen as an attempt to provide an articulate framework to interpret our cognitive experience. It will try to show how our theoretical endeavors are sustained throughout by our pre-articulate personal appropriation of them. The impersonal and objective claims of all our theoretical or formal expressions are grounded in our personal acceptance of them. In order to validate this personal knowledge, then, we must show that it can transcend the personal level to this universal level, all the while retaining its personal ground. Writing from the vantage point of existential phenomenology, one author succinctly expressed the problem in this way:

> A concrete person. . .is neither the dark brooding core of Kierkegaardian existence nor the universal consciousness of Husserl. He is, rather, the continuous interplay of these two factors which, taken in themselves, appear to exclude one another. How, then, are we to clarify this unity?[48]

Polanyi's theory claims to clarify this unity and by so doing to validate this activity which constitutes our knowledge of reality.

This explication of the process and scope which is required for the validation of human knowing should have made it clear that this effort cannot be limited to the remarks contained in the concluding sections of this chapter. In a real

sense the attempt to validate personal knowledge started with
the critique of the critical-objective stance as the only
legitimate way of understanding human knowing, and it assumed
greater force in the introductory description of Polanyi's proposals. Now, during the forthcoming study of our personal appropriation of experience and its interpretation through symbolic systems and development through a historical unfolding,
the personal elements of validation will be examined. Then
the process will continue finally by encompassing an appraisal
of the status of what our knowledge is about. Only when we
have reached this stage can the outlines of how personal knowledge is validated be understood. An indispensable requirement
in order for this to occur, however, is that the reader must
follow the developing interpretation as it unfolds through an
examination of his own personal conscious activity. Our hope
is that eventually this will issue in the reader's recognition
of Polanyi's theory of personal knowledge as validated in his
own conscious experience, or at least as a possible way of understanding his experience. Finally, from this foundational
reorganization of our intellectual activity, we shall be in a
position to understand more clearly the meaning and significance of religious belief.

2. Personal indwelling

The critical problem facing us focuses on how we can uphold our understanding of our experiences if our personal participation is a determinant of all our acts of explicit knowledge. Since our knowledge has this tacit base, our course
of action must begin by analyzing how this tacit power functions. To rely solely on analysis of our explicit forms of
thought is to avoid the more painstaking self-reflection on
our responsible judgments about reality, perhaps for the sake
of the illusory security provided by the impersonal certain-
ties fostered by our modern cultural heritage. A foundational
inquiry into the human mode of knowing cannot be satisfied
with this.

We may begin our inquiry by considering our ordinary perception of things. It is a regular occurrence for us to recognize coherent shapes or physiognomies out of the myriad sensa-

tions that constantly beset our eyes and other sense organs. Beyond simple types of this achievement, some of us have studied to heighten our perceptual powers to include more accomplished forms of recognition, such as diagnosing maladies or appreciating good art. And yet the means for accomplishing these activities we normally do not--and often cannot--explicitly clarify. Even if we do express how we come to perceive something, the expression temporarily halts the perception and is usually for the benefit of someone else. But then the effort of the other person to attempt to see the object in light of our explanation is assumed. This is an example of Polanyi's contention that we know more than we can tell even in our perceptions.

In his efforts to explain this phenomenon, Polanyi has taken a cue from the findings of Gestalt psychologists.[49] He does not, however, regard the achievement of the comprehension of a pattern as a completely passive experience. Rather, he holds that this is an active integration achieved by our tacit powers. He thus avoids the difficulties inherent in many modern philosophical explanations that attempt to regard sensory awareness as a completely passive experience.[50] Our coherent perceptions are the result of our active shaping of experience through the dynamic orientation of ourselves to reality. Such active integrations are achieved by our tacit powers which sustain all our discoveries and accredit them as true.

There have been many psychological studies done on the level of subliminal awareness which provide a quantitative demonstration of an elementary form of tacit knowing.[51] A process termed "subception" by psychologists has been interpreted by Polanyi as an example of how we tacitly acquire our knowledge. The experimental situation consists in a slight electric shock being administered to a subject after a specific kind of nonsense syllable within a whole set of such syllables. In a period of time the subject anticipated the shock whenever the specific "shock syllable" appeared. Yet he could not identify it when questioned by the experimenter.

This reveals the basic elements of tacit knowing and how we can know more than we can tell. Two terms are involved. The first, or *distal* term,[52] is focally known. In this case, the electric shock. The second, or *proximal* term, is subsidiarily known by relying on it for attending to something else. Again, in the example of subception the proximal term consists in the shock syllable.

We are drawing closer now to an understanding of how Polanyi interprets these psychological observations by developing them into the elements of his theory of knowledge. This model of our perception, as a simplified illustration of tacit knowing, provides the connective link between our bodily processes and our higher forms of creative thought.[53] We can trace this through an analysis of our performance of an act of comprehension.[54]

Whenever understanding occurs, comprehension has been achieved. This means a formerly disconnected set of particular elements has been shifted so that the way in which we are aware of the particulars becomes altered: we now are aware of them only in terms of the whole. We have a subsidiary awareness of the particulars and a focal awareness of the whole. This distinction is not precisely parallel to the distinction between tacit and explicit knowledge, but should be considered as a further clarification of tacit knowing itself.[55]

Throughout all our acts of comprehension we are dependent on our bodily processes. Our body is the means by which we gain intellectual and practical control over our surroundings. We rely on the physiological functions of our body as they encounter external objects which stimulate them by integrating and projecting these internal experiences in the form of a focally meaningful comprehension. Even though we are not focally aware of the internal process of our central nervous system, the scope of our tacit knowing includes this.[56] It is in this radical sense, then, that Polanyi claims that all thought has a bodily basis: we normally are aware of our body only subsidiarily because we experience it in terms of the world to which we are focally attending.

This is in fact the way we use tools, as our earlier discussion anticipated. When we properly use a tool, we rely on it subsidiarily to focus on the whole activity in which the tool is employed. It comes to function as an extension of our senses, because we rely on our bodily sensations of the external world as mediated by the tool, and effectively incorporate it into our body. Thus by making a tool function as a proximal term of our tacit knowing, we dwell in it similarly to the way we dwell in our body. Through our active integration of these particulars we comprehend the tool in a meaningful fashion by focally attending to the act which constitutes the distal term of our tacit knowing.

Such indwelling may now be further generalized to include our intelligent use of conceptual systems. We rely on a naturalist view of the world, for example, by interiorizing it. When we dwell in such a system, it functions as a tacit framework from which we attend to certain things which are seen in its light. The indwelling whereby we interiorize a conceptual system is again analogous to the way we dwell in our bodies.[57] Tacit knowing may now be understood as an indwelling through which we interiorize certain elements of our experience in order to be aware of them in terms of our focal attention on the comprehensive entity they constitute. Two significant points follow from this.

First, the understanding of tacit knowing in the framework of indwelling clarifies the meaning of Polanyi's thesis that knowing is something we do. Since the very possibility of our experiencing anything at all is dependent on our tacit integration of its particulars, all our knowledge is sustained by some sort of personal achievement. Our knowledge, in other words, is not simply a passive experience: we do not simply "look at the facts" as though "facts" did something called "facting" to us. Rather, we must act upon our experience by interiorizing its elements, by expanding ourselves into the world to dwell in these particulars, and finally by shaping them in order to focus on their joint meaning.

Knowing as doing, further, explains why Polanyi stresses discovery as the paradigm case of knowledge. It is fairly well established that we must learn to see things. In general all our acts of perception, most of which have become routine by childhood, exhibit on an impoverished level the same structure as the richly provocative insights of creative imagination. Since in perception we tacitly integrate particulars to focus on the whole which they constitute, we constantly expand

ourselves into the world. As the indwelling of some becomes
more profound, they are enabled to create new modes of appreciating external reality. The groping achievement of an infant's
new perception is thus similar in structure to the creative
probings of those who advance the frontiers of knowledge. What
is casually achieved in ordinary perception is dramatically
portrayed in great discoveries.[58]

Since all our attempts to understand reality issue from
our active participation in the knowing process, it follows
that the way this is performed will shape the knower in its
turn. Every act of understanding modifies the way we exist in
the world. Whenever we come to a new recognition, we interiorize the particulars and enlarge our mental being by learning to
rely on an ever-increasing set of particulars. This is particularly significant when there is a question of a shift in
tacit framework. Such a move would radically alter our way of
being, depending on its degree of intensity--as is the claim
in religious conversion.[59]

The second point, which follows from the recognition that
knowing is a form of doing, is that the dichotomies which
plague many theories of knowledge are transcended. There is
no discontinuity, for example, between the study of nature and
the study of man.[60] Our ability to understand through indwelling is operative, contrary to Dilthey's formulation,[61] in the
sciences just as much as in history. This does not mean that
there are no specific differences in methodology between various disciplines. Polanyi is speaking of our knowledge on the
fundamental level of its pervading structure. It is only upon
this that we may formulate methods appropriate for dealing with
various segments of our experience. From this foundational
vantage point the participation of the knower in that which he
knows is seen to form a continuum. Greater participation is
required in loving a person than in analyzing the chemical
makeup of a rock, just as the former modifies a person in a
way that the latter cannot do. Yet the difference is one of
degree, not kind. The dynamic structure underlying both is
the same.

This implies that the recognition of knowing as doing
transcends the fact/value dichotomy prevalent in much of modern

thought. By now it should be clear that all our "factual" judgments are dependent on our prior tacit integration of particulars. How we achieve this integration is an evaluative judgment on our part and is not derivable from any simplistic analysis of the "facts." No matter how "objective" or "value-free" any statement of fact may appear to be, such a statement is possible only if some prior form of appraisal has been made. It is this prior appraisal which allows us to entertain certain elements of our experience as "facts." In every affirmation, therefore, both factual and evaluative components contribute to our act of knowing.[62] Their relationship can again be seen to form a continuum where differences will consist in degree of stress on one or the other, not a difference of kind implying the absence of one or the other.

The panorama of knowledge thus opened sees man as a responsible agent shaping all that he knows in his efforts at mastering his environment. This dynamism impels men ever forward in their search for a more adequate understanding of their experience. Such understanding through comprehension, while an eminently personal affair, is not thereby merely subjective. For as we come to dwell meaningfully in the world, we make ourselves in relation to the world in a particular fashion which we judge to be valid. This judgment is, of course, contingent and always open to development and modification. Yet the judgment transcends the individual who asserts it because *its intent is universal*.[63] Granted that another person comes to share our comprehension, our affirmations claim that he, too, will accept it as true. Our responsible judgments made within the context of our personal indwelling provide one pole of the validation of our knowledge. The reality, to which our judgment is united by our tacit knowledge, will provide the external pole.[64] For the moment we shall continue our probings by expanding our analysis of personal indwelling to include an understanding of our ability to use symbols meaningfully and of our development of them in time. Hopefully this preliminary indication of how our personal knowledge is validated through our universal intent will correspondingly become clearer.

3. Linguistic indwelling

The primary way in which we interpret our experience is by means of our conceptual symbols. By incorporating an articulate framework into our bodily existence, we become capable of extending the range of our experience far beyond our pre-articulate faculties. Linguistic indwelling provides us with a ready storehouse for ordering and shaping our experience. How we come to use words, which is a distinctively human trait, has long been a puzzle for philosophical inquiry. It is Polanyi's contention that by understanding this process as a further instance of tacit knowing we will be provided with a cogent interpretation of how we may rely validly on the use of our linguistic powers.[65]

Understanding is an achievement through which we integrate tacitly our bodily processes in order to focus on an external object. When we endow things with meaning we interiorize them and subsidiarily rely on them for focally attending to their joint meaning. If, on the other hand, we exteriorize something or alienate it from ourselves, we destroy its meaning for us. For example, if we focus on a word it becomes a meaningless babble or a series of blotches on paper. Only when the word functions subsidiarily, that is, only when we attend from the word to the meaning it signifies, does it become meaningful and lose its external opaqueness.[66]

The identification of consecutive levels of meaning and sequences of integration which normally function in our efforts at communication throws more light on the problem of language. A speech is an expression of meaningful sounds, which form words, which grammatically make up a sentence and stylistically constitute, for example, a eulogy. The speaker is involved in an act of sense-giving by controlling a hierarchy of meaningful levels where each level functions subsidiarily to the next higher level and the whole act is composed of a series of integrations. A member of the audience is involved in an act of sense-reading in which he subsidiarily integrates the levels of meaning into the focal experience of understanding the speech. Through such sense-giving and sense-reading we produce and understand the meaning of a text without focally knowing the text itself.[67]

A similar structural differentiation is observable between an immediate experience and the verbal communication of it. The understanding of someone's report of an immediate experience is an act of sense-reading, just as is his comprehension of the immediate experience. Yet they differ because in the latter case the experience is an act of sense-reading which incorporates particulars and tacitly integrates them into a focal whole, while in the former instance of sense-reading (mediated through the sense-giving act of the person's production of the report) the meaning is grasped through our reliance on the words alone. Thus when we experience something, the meaning is immediately present, whereas the meaning of the original experience expressed verbally is present only in thought. This shows, further, how our use of language can go beyond a physical object to one that is less tangible. In these cases, such as a discussion about a "just" society, our focal attention is bearing upon a more purely mental object by subsidiarily integrating the proximal particulars of our experience on a more profound level. In this way the theory of tacit knowing resolves the conflict concerning denotative language between modern and classical views by admitting possible references for our words to both objects and conceptions and by holding a continuity between the two.[68]

The acceptance of this possibility, however, requires an adequate explanation of the traditional philosophical problem of universal terms.[69] The problem consists in the recognition that when we apply a universal term, the objects which we thus identify differ from each other in all their particular cases. Whether we would hold that the universal has a reality beyond the world, or that it is merely a name for a collection of things in a class, or that it has an open-texture which allows for differences in application, the problem still remains. These historical proposals still do not explain how the universal term is properly applied to some objects or situations and not others.

These difficulties have prevailed because they all seek explicit procedures to explain how we subsume a particular into a class. Polanyi's account, on the other hand, holds that our use of universal terms is dependent on a tacit integration

of particulars such as we have seen operating in perception.
Through a present tacit integration formed in conjunction with
a multitude of past experiences we are enabled to form a conception, even though the particulars may be contradictory in
themselves. The reality of universals consists in their joint
meaning of all those things or qualities which contribute to
it and their capability of being manifested indefinitely in
the future.[70]

This also explains how words have any meaning at all.
Any attempt to account for the meaning of words as "sounds"
corresponding to "objects" according to some set of rules does
not work for the simple reason that the effort at joining them
requires the same sort of integration the explanation was supposed to provide. Similarly meaning understood as habitual
association of sounds with objects implies that both are equally focal. But this would negate the intentional or vectorial
quality of the words whereby we attend from the word to the
meaning it conveys.[71] Moreover we have already seen that we
are focally unaware of the word itself, but that if we do become so aware the word is exteriorized and loses its meaning.
Only by regarding our intelligent use of speech as an instance
of sense-giving and sense-reading can we comprehend how language is meaningful: "The relation of a word to that which it
denotes is established by a tacit integration in which we rely
on a subsidiary awareness of the word for directing our attention to its meaning."[72] This integration removes the word from
its status as an opaque external entity by interiorizing it as
part of our bodily endowment, thereby allowing it to function
as an intelligible form for reading our experience and giving
it a particular meaning.

These preliminary clarifications will now allow us to
consider two crucial problems of linguistics.[73] Briefly stated, they concern how a child can learn to use a language, including the profound logic of the language, and how we can
understand and compose completely novel sentences. By analyzing these difficulties from the vantage point of the dynamic
activity of knowing, Polanyi has thrown considerable light on
our use of language and the functioning of symbols.

The proposal by which Polanyi would account for these

problems has already been anticipated in the discussion of knowing as discovery. We have seen how a problem arises in response to our creative powers which tacitly or intuitively begin to grasp a coherence which is as yet hidden from focal awareness. The creative imagination then strains for new clues to be integrated tacitly. As the coherence gradually begins to form we continue to probe with our intuition and imaginatively create new conceptions to describe the emerging coherence. This deepening coherence guides our tacit probings and imaginative evocations of new conceptions until our tacit integrations progressively become more focal. Finally a judgment is made whereby the coherence, which was at first known intuitively or tacitly, has emerged into a new meaningful insight. Such is the process of heuristics grounded in tacit knowing.

Similarly this provides a model for explaining how we are able to learn a language and use it effectively. Our reliance on a linguistic system is a tacit activity in which we integrate the particulars of words and grammar into a comprehensive whole which gradually becomes more coherent as we progress in our use of the language. Thus as soon as a child learns to rely on even a minimum of words, he interiorizes along with them some elemental rules of grammar. From then on the mutual efforts of his imagination and intuition combine to provide a growth in vocabulary and a correspondingly greater precision in the application of grammar. This takes place in the child along with a host of complementary achievements, such as conceptions of stable objects, spatial and causal relations, and the personality of individual people.

All these considerations provide a basis for the validity of our linguistic indwelling. The seeming paradox, that in order to have one concept we must somehow have them all, is resolved by the recognition that the system of language and the logic of its grammar is a tacit achievement. Like an achievement in the proficiency of a skill, language is acquired by a tacit integration. Consequently it can be expanded constantly to cover new and unique experiences even though we are focally ignorant of the explicit rules according to which this is performed. This places the dynamics of our use of language on a heuristic level, which is exemplified in our application of

universal terms.[74] Just as a universal term can anticipate
future instances with an indefinite range of properties, so too
our language as a whole can expand and grow to meet our ever
developing search for fuller understanding. Inherent in our
personal and linguistic indwellings is thus a recognition of
the contingency and historical rootedness of all our knowing.

4. Historical indwelling

Tacit knowing, by the very fact that it is an activity, is
fundamentally historical. Unlike the objectivist ideal of impersonal, critical detachment of the absolute choice of an isolated subject, tacit knowing is an achievement which comprehends both universal intent and personal responsibility in a
continuous process of mutual growth. By retracing some previously discussed elements of tacit knowing from the vantage
point of their involvement in time, the meaning and scope of
our historical indwelling will emerge along with Polanyi's proposal for appreciating its validity.

In our analysis of perception the basic structure of our
tacit knowing was described as a subsidiary reliance on particulars which we integrate into a focal whole. Our knowledge
is directed *from* the proximal term *to* the distal. Through this
process we interiorize elements of the world into ourselves,
and we then reach out from ourselves into the world in the form
of focal awareness. Our awareness of an object includes,
therefore, our reliance on a "background." Whenever we perceive some object, we must first tacitly assume a background,
in which for the moment we dwell, so that the object may be
meaningfully situated.[75] This background, or horizon,[76] comprises the context of all our knowing and by personal effort
may be expanded as the need arises. Our horizons can thus be
extended indefinitely to include an infinite range of tacitly
held particulars.

From this vantage point we can see how every act of perception is achieved through a duration of time. Out of the
maze of objects and relations which might possibly comprise the
focus of our attention, we act first by interiorizing certain
elements so that they may contribute (along with linguistic and
cultural components) in forming the tacit horizon of our place

in the world. From within this horizon, we move on by relying on some particular elements in order to attend from them to an identifiable object or activity. Our acts of perception are thus a reaching out of ourselves from our self-constitution achieved in the past into the focal point of our attention which draws us toward the future. In the continuously present activity of perceiving external reality we are reshaping ourselves by expanding our horizons in order to focus on new possibilities foreshadowed in the current achievement.

A similar directedness in time can be observed in our linguistic indwelling. Aside from the fact that we must learn the language we speak--an activity obviously performed over a period of time, the very use of a language is conditioned upon its involvement in time. Our language, or some particular sphere of it, constitutes a conceptual system which provides a formal intelligibility through its definitions of categories and causal relationships. In order for us to recognize a "fact," we must tacitly rely on the system and the formal intelligibility it confers by focusing our attention from it (and other tacitly held elements) to the object. Then we can make an intelligent judgment, such as "This is a desk." All of this implies that when we rely on our language to refer to something in an existential judgment, the resulting affirmation is, to use the traditional notion, "synthetic a priori."[77] It is so, however, in a way which a man of the Enlightenment would not grasp. For while Polanyi would agree that our formal lingustiic systems expand the range of our tacit powers immeasurably by providing the chief source of intelligibility for understanding our experience of the world, he also insists that the present conceptual systems conveyed through our language are not ultimate. Because of the constant probing of our tacit powers into as yet unthought-of possible experiences, the realm of actual experience available to us through our reliance on a conceptual system may gradually expand beyond the intelligibility originally provided by the system. As a result the pressure of new discoveries may gradually alter or, in some instances, radically change any historically situated framework. In short, our "synthetic a prioris" change.[78]

Finally our historical indwelling may be extended to

include the entire expanse of horizons which comprise human thought. By dwelling in our cultural heritage, the past achievements of mankind serve as the repository of our standards and the criteria for judging reality. In the final analysis this reliance defines our mode of existence and our view of reality. Since this radical historical setting is the ultimate ground for the unfolding of our thought, its eradication is an impossibility. Even if an individual claims to have transcended a particular horizon in his area of competence by means of a new discovery, his breakthrough could have been achieved only within the matrix originally defined by the horizon.

Unfortunately, as soon as the historical, and therefore contingent, foundations of human knowledge are acknowledged, the ugly monster of absolute subjectivism and relativism seems to rear its head. For if our knowledge unfolds through a tacit reliance on a conceptual system, and if, as we have indicated earlier,[79] the stability of conceptual systems is not an automatic guarantee of its truth, how can we call our understanding of the world anything more than a convention generally agreed upon in one particular culture at one particular time? The import of this question can be seen more thoroughly by clarifying the complex network of interrelated problems which it raises.

Within the context of the historical unfolding of knowledge there are four significant possibilities for judging the validity of human activity: (1) valid reasoning performed within a true system, (2) incorrect conclusions drawn from a true system, (3) rational inferences derived from a fallacious framework, and (4) irrational and incoherent actions as in pathological cases.[80] Polanyi's claim, of course, is that we can achieve the situation described by (1). Before we consider it, however, it would be helpful to clarify the three fallacies which can occur in our assessment of historical activity.[81]

In (2) we apply our own standards to different epochs without regard for the intellectual framework within which the individuals were performing their activity. By failing to recognize the cultural determinants of the society, this type of reasoning draws incorrect conclusions about the age in question from a framework accepted as true. Polanyi terms this

the rationalist fallacy, a tendency observable in such eight-
eenth century authors as Gibbon and Voltaire.

The consistent application of case (4) to historical activity usually requires a materialist or reductivist conception
of man, including his knowledge and the aspirations expressed
in it. Here all supposedly human activity is understood to be
the result of some type of antecedent mechanical causes. An
explanation of this sort deems any sense of rationality inherent to man as illusory. This manner of judging historical
action Polanyi calls the determinist fallacy.

Probably the most vexing of these errors occurs in (3),
perhaps because the effects of the prime exemplar of its application, known as historicism, are still with us. The actions of men here are judged solely by the standards of their
own time. If pushed to its logical conclusions this approach
errs in sanctioning an absolute conformity by requiring every-
one to do no more than operate out of his cultural horizons.
This is the relativist fallacy, which maintains that men cannot go beyond the horizons prescribed by their cultural situations and must be judged accordingly, even if the horizon be
erroneous.

In order to avoid the relativist fallacy, we must acknowledge that case (1) is possible. Great care must be exercised,
however, in delimiting what such a claim entails. It does not
mean that our present cultural horizons embody the fullness of
truth, the implications of which we may simply deduce by some
logical procedure. Nor does it quite mean that it has grapsed
some "truths" which are now forever accessible to man because
of their absolute and unchanging character, and that the task
remaining consists in discovering the "rest" of these truths.
Such proposals would ignore the historical rootedness of our
knowledge. Moreover, since implicitly they limit the notion
of truth to explicit formulations, they would have difficulty
in accounting for the contingent character of all explicit
affirmations which result from their grounding in a developing
tacitly held horizon.

The claim, that we can operate correctly within a valid
framework, implies simply that our reliance on the ultimate
tacit horizons which describe our cultural heritage provides

an adequate frame of reference for our understanding of reality. Through our cultural indwelling we have an access to truth which enables us to go beyond the historical limits outlined in our explicit affirmations of this truth. As long as our society continues to foster the ideals embodied in its cultural tradition in such a way that it encourages creativity and novelty in the pursuit of ever more adequate expressions of the truth, we may have confidence that we are moving in the right direction, not that we are already there. Because of our reliance on the tacit grounds of our thought, we have criteria, albeit at the most profound level unformalized, for judging the degree of validity entailed in other cultural expressions and in competing views within our own culture. Any one individual, of course, possesses only a limited access to his cultural heritage, and this circumscribes his field of competence or "calling." In this way the society as a whole recognizes that its individual members may exercise their intrinsic powers of thought in their areas of competence, so that, by learning from insights of other cultures or through probing the implications in their own culture, they may affirm new discoveries which may in turn lead to the overthrow of the tacit frame of reference which originally allowed them to discern the problem. When we affirm this as our ultimate aim--that individuals can rely on their cultural background as a basis for probing the frontiers of knowledge in responsible dedication to the truth and that once they discover something they affirm it with universal intent--then we have described the foundations of a "society of explorers."[82]

There is a sense in which some may still feel a bit uneasy with such an ultimate justification for the holding of our knowledge. Such uneasiness is understandable, for, as Polanyi points out, our intellectual heritage "comprises everything in which we may be totally mistaken."[83] But this merely describes the risk in being alive. The apprehension, then, is perhaps partially due to what we have described as our accustomed reliance on the illusory security provided by an objectivist view of knowledge with its seemingly "automatic" or "logically compelling" understanding of reality, thereby minimizing or totally exempting the knower from any active responsibility in his judgments.

Yet the misgiving may not be this at all. For one may be quite willing to accept the element of risk involved in knowing and still question the validity of personal knowledge. The problem may be expressed in this way: in spite of the demands of responsibility, the recognition that the human mode of knowing requires the intervention of the knowing subject in every affirmation may still seem, if no longer capricious or subjective, then perhaps "phenomenal." The problem thus requires an explanation of this crucial point: how does the process which sustains our responsible judgments made with universal intent issue in a knowledge of reality? The following observations will help in understanding what this problem involves.

A society of explorers describes man in thought. The actual meaning of the cultural tradition within which we dwell is complemented by the potential meaning its historical development will reveal through human effort.[84] This process whereby the gradient of discovery is activated may be understood through the concept of a heuristic field.[85] In this situation we rely on our frameworks of thought to guide us to ever more adequate comprehensions of reality. While the ultimate standards of a conceptual system in effect at any particular time are only tacitly known, secondary criteria may, through reflection, be explicitly formulated from this tacit base. In the process of making a new discovery or opening a new horizon, the creative effort is guided partly by our tacit and explicit criteria and partly by the object under investigation. The achievement of a discovery, in addition to the explicit claims, leads often to a tacit acceptance of new standards of coherence or new values. In the action of achieving this breakthrough, we have tacitly assumed new criteria which we now accredit in the act of proclaiming the discovery with universal intent. This means that the base of our dwelling in the world has expanded. The process may begin again when the new insight stimulates further reflection which may lead to new formulations of explicit criteria established in the newly accepted tacit grounds. These may eventually provide both a justification of the discovery and at the same time an impetus for another individual to push the quest further.[86]

The critical element in this explication is that we do indeed know reality. The explanation of the process whereby we tacitly change or modify our criteria can function *only if* the advance is based on reality. Otherwise there would be no way of accounting for such a shift in values. Polanyi clearly expresses the conviction that in order for our tacit knowing to permit us to go beyond our formalized expressions, as it in fact does, it must be grounded in the real.

> We can account for this capacity of ours to know more than we can tell if we believe in the presence of an external reality with which we can establish contact. This I do. I declare myself committed to the belief in an external reality gradually accessible to knowing, and I regard all true understanding as an intimation of such a reality which, being real, may yet reveal itself to our deepened understanding in an indefinite range of manifestations. I accept the obligation to search for the truth through my own intimations of reality, knowing that there is, and can be, no strict rule by which my conclusions can be justified. My reference to reality legitimates my acts of unspecifiable knowing, even while it duly keeps the exercise of such acts within the bounds of a rational objectivity. For a claim to have made contact with reality necessarily legislates both for myself and others with universal intent.[87]

Tacit knowing thus has two aspects: the responsible act of judgment which is its personal pole, and the meaning of objective reality expressed in true statements with universal intent which is its external pole.[88] Because the tacit ground of our thought links our explicit professions of the truth with the reality to which they refer, the human mode of knowing must always be personal in order for it to be objective.

The task before us now consists in providing a validation for the claim that an affirmation made with universal intent not only satisfies the demands of our mode of knowing--which has hopefully been satisfactorily demonstrated--but that it is also in some sense objective. We are faced, in short, with the problem of metaphysical knowledge.

NOTES TO CHAPTER III

1. The substance of this appraisal, but with a different emphasis, may be found in Bernard Longergan, "Theology and Man's Future," *Cross Currents*, XIX (1969), 455. For some of the relevant passages from Aristotle, see the *Posterior Analytics* I, 1, 71b 10-12; I, 2, 71b 25 and 72a 37f; I, 33, 88b, 30f.

2. "Problem Solving," 89.

3. "The Creative Imagination," 85.

4. That this is so can be seen negatively from the harshly critical review of *Knowing and Being* by Anthony Manser in *Philosophical Books*, XI (May, 1970), 21-23. Written from an objectivist viewpoint, this review correctly recognizes that the indeterminacy involved in discovery is a crucial element of Polanyi's understanding of knowledge, but then does not adequately grasp the import of this point. Because of his objectivist standpoint, Manser completely misinterprets Polanyi's understanding of the role of the scientific community by asserting "apparently Galileo would have been more firmly dealt with by Polanyi than by the Church" (p. 22). Aside from the astonishingly naive and historically simplistic equation of the role of the scientific community with the role of Church in Galileo's time which Manser--quite incorrectly--implies is part of Polanyi's position, he still looks for some "publicly verifiable method of dealing with the claims of scientists." Polanyi's contention is simply that what counts as "publicly verifiable" is determined for science by scientists. Until this is grasped one is still within an objectivist framework and may agree easily with Manser's assessment of the theory of tacit knowledge as "bankrupt."

5. "Problem Solving," 92.

6. For Copernicus, see Polanyi's discussion of the many *ad hoc* assumptions and the mechanical objections to the basis of his theory in "The Creative Imagination," 86. For Kepler, see Polanyi's analysis of his mystical Pythagorean assumptions as his rationale for the heliocentric theory in *Personal Knowledge*, p. 7.

7. *Critique of Pure Reason*, A 133, translated by F. Max Muller (Garden City, N.Y.: Doubleday & Co., Inc., Anchor Books, 1966), p. 119. See also Kant's observations concerning the application of the schemata of understanding to particular cases of phenomena as "an art hidden in the depth of the human soul, the true secrets of which we shall hardly ever be able to guess and reveal" (A 141; Anchor edition, p. 123). Polanyi refers to the Kantian insights several times in his later articles. See, in *Knowing and Being*, "The Unaccountable Element in Science," pp. 105-106, "Knowing and Being," p. 133, and "Sense-Giving and Sense-Reading," p. 191.

8. "Pure and Applied Science and their Appropriate Forms of Organization," *Dialectica*, X (1956), 233.

9. *Science, Faith and Society*, p. 14.

10. Marjorie Grene, *The Knower and the Known*, p. 159.

11. See "On the Introduction of Science into Moral Subjects," 203-204.

12. See Polanyi's prolonged argument and series of illustrations in Part I of *Personal Knowledge*, "The Art of Knowing," particularly the example of crystallography, pp. 43-48.

13. See above p. 43, where we indicated that his proposal to understand knowledge as being of two kinds was first expressed in Chapter 4, "Skills," of *Personal Knowledge* (pp. 49-65). The present discussion is based primarily on this chapter. For his more comprehensive and later explanation of the structure and aspects involved in the theory of tacit knowing, see below Chapter IV, Section A, "The Structure of Tacit Knowing."

14. Carl Michalson, for example, in *The Rationality of Faith* (New York: Charles Scribner's Sons, 1963), considers Polanyi's ideas "an excellent antidote to the myth of positivism in natural science" (p. 37), but feels all efforts at ending the bifurcation between nature and history are unconvincing (p. 35). Ultimately this is due to Michalson's acceptance of the Kantian distinction between theoretical and practical reason (see pp. 25-26 and 46) or, as he would prefer to put it, between reality as judged by the structure of history and the structure of nature--a methodological dichotomy (p. 31). With this prior conceptual frame, he reads Polanyi's insistence on the personal factor in science as "some lag or some distortion in the perceptual responses of the experimenter" (p. 36). This is, of course, a possible interpretation, especially for many of the examples Polanyi adduces. But insofar as they are meant to illustrate the tacit component of knowing, the examples are intended by Polanyi to point beyond themselves to the interrelated structure operating in the act of knowing. Because of his preconceptions, however, Michalson cannot see these further aspects and regards them as basically no more personal than being nearsighted.

15. "Knowing and Being," 123.

16. *Personal Knowledge*, p. 58.

17. *Ibid.*, p. 61.

18. Except where otherwise noted the source for most of the thought expressed in this section, including the critical documentation of the experimental studies upon which some of it is based, is Chapters 5 and 6 of *Personal Knowledge*.

Our presentation will attempt primarily to trace the logic of Polanyi's position.

19. See *The Study of Man*, pp. 14-17.

20. *Ibid.*, p. 25.

21. "Sense-Giving and Sense-Reading," p. 187. For contemporary examples of philosophical reflection acknowledging the preconceptual grasp of reality, see Karl Rahner, *Spirit in the World*, trans. by William Dych (New York: Herder & Herder, 1968), pp. 67ff and Bernard Lonergan, *Insight* (New York: Philosophical Library, 1958), pp. 272f.

22. "Pure and Applied Science and Their Appropriate Forms of Organization," 232-233.

23. "Problem Solving," 98.

24. See "The Creative Imagination," 88-92.

25. "Problem Solving," 102.

26. See *Personal Knowledge*, p. 162.

27. *Personal Knowledge*, pp. 204-209; see also "Sense-Giving and Sense-Reading," pp. 185-187.

28. This is a common theme with Polanyi, which is quite understandable considering that it is out of his work on the defense of science as a community in pursuit of truth that he developed his theory of personal knowledge. For some of Polanyi's ideas on this, see *The Logic of Liberty*, Part I; *Science, Faith and Society*, Chapters II and III; in *Knowing and Being*, "The Republic of Science," pp. 49-72 and "The Growth of Science in Society, pp. 73-86; and *The Tacit Dimension*, Chapter 3.

29. *Science, Faith and Society*, p. 56.

30. "The Republic of Science," pp. 65-66. The fact that some subtle external influences affect the functioning of certain aspects of the scientific community (e.g., if a scientist's work is useful in "defense," he may get a bigger government grant; or with the current emphasis on ecology environmentalists may be in greater demand and thus be a more attractive field to aspiring scientists) does not thereby detract from the authority of science; it merely shows that the scientist is also a member of a larger cultural community and shares its values too. This is clarified, in *Science, Faith and Society*, pp. 56-60, by Polanyi's distinction between a General Authority laying down presuppositions but then demanding freedom under them and a Specific Authority imposing conclusions irrespective of the mind of its constituents. The former he attributes to science and a free society in general, the latter he attributes, perhaps too simplistically, to Roman Catholicism and later in the work by implication

to totalitarianism. From this perspective it is thus clear that, unless government or culture dictates conclusions to science, it is not abrogating the internal authority of science even though it may suggest or direct current preoccupations.

31. *Science, Faith and Society*, p. 54.

32. "The Republic of Science," pp. 55-56.

33. See *Science, Faith and Society*, pp. 47-50, for a brief description of these controls.

34. *The Tacit Dimension*, pp. 71-73.

35. *Science, Faith and Society*, p. 28, "The Growth of Science in Society," p. 79, and *The Tacit Dimension*, pp. 75-76. Polanyi's contention that science remains continuous in the face of revolutionary paradigm shifts appears to be a major disagreement with Kuhn's thesis, even though they generally agree in other matters. The discontinuity that Kuhn seems to stress is perhaps due to his emphasis on looking at the discovery before the event when the course of history is still indeterminate. But if one looks from well after the fact, scientific growth may appear to be almost predetermined (as the text-book view often has it). Polanyi tries to hold on to both elements by recognizing that there are intimations contained in present knowledge while at the same time recognizing that they are only intimations and need the personal intervention of creative minds to bring them to light. In this way he preserves the continuity of the scientific community while recognizing the real breakthrough of major revolutionary insights.

36. See above p. 21.

37. For the discussion which follows, see *Personal Knowledge*, pp. 286-294 and "The Stability of Beliefs," 27-37. The latter has been substantially incorporated into the former.

38. At this point in our analysis we wish only to expose the problem of relativism with respect to cultural frameworks. The foundational problem of explaining how we may uphold our knowledge of reality even though it is expressed through historically conditioned frameworks will be outlined below in the last section of Chapter IV, "D. The Discovery of Reality."

39. "The Creative Imagination," 91.

40. Our point here is reminiscent of Newman's distinction between "certainty" as a quality of propositions and "certitude" as a mental state and his further contention that certitude is not a passive experience but the active recognition of concrete truth. Since, according to Newman, this cannot result from abstract, formal reasoning, the sole criterion of the accuracy of an inference in

concrete matters leading to certitude is the human mind operating through its "Illative Sense." See John Henry Newman, *An Essay in Aid of a Grammar of Assent* (Garden City, N.Y.: Doubleday & Company, Inc., Image Books, 1955), Chapter Nine, "The Illative Sense," especially pp. 271, 275, and 281. It should be indicated here that Polanyi's analysis will eventually go beyond Newman's. While Newman is content simply to acknowledge and insist upon the importance of the personal judgment in all matters of truth, Polanyi tries to explain, as we shall see below, the structures of our tacit operations which provides an understanding of the grounds of our certitude.

41. As we had already seen above, this is a crucial juncture at which Polanyi diverges from objectivist and most language-analysis positions. If the empirically observable processes which constitute the mechanical operations of the brain totally account for the phenomenon of "thought," then a behaviorist examination and description of the neural interactions is the only legitimate way to approach what Polanyi is calling for. Again, if we must analyze the explicit uses of language in order to avoid specious problems which arise when language is idling, then the "experience" of thinking is properly described only by examining how language in fact is used. This is, I believe, the significance of Wittgenstein's "idling engine" metaphor and the import of many of his other observations. See for example secs. 132, 318-321, 426-429, and IIxi (pp. 219e-220e) of *Philosophical Investigations* (New York: The Macmillan Company, 1953). Yet it should be noted that some recent commentators on the later Wittgenstein propose surprising similarities in methods and results with Polanyi; see C. B. Daly, "Polanyi and Wittgenstein," in *Intellect and Hope*, pp. 136-168 and Jerry H. Gill, *The Possibility of Religious Knowledge* (Grand Rapids, Mich.: William B. Eerdmans Publishing Company, 1971).

42. "The Hypothesis of Cybernetics," *The British Journal for the Philosophy of Science*, II (1952), 313.

43. *The Tacit Dimension*, p. 87.

44. "The Creative Imagination," 85. Polanyi thus takes issue with the impersonal implications of the principle of falsification as set forth by Karl Popper in *The Logic of Scientific Discovery* (New York: Harper & Row, 1959). Here Popper asserts that "we try to prove that our anticipations were false" (p. 279), in an attempt to stress that our discoveries are not simply the result of prejudices. Popper's intention is certainly commendable, but his desire for an impersonal method for attaining it leads to very strange conclusions, to say the least. The creative anticipation of a scientist, Polanyi affirms to the contrary, "*risks* defeat but never *seeks* it; it is in fact his craving for success that makes the scientist take the risk of failure." See *The Tacit Dimension*, pp. 79 and 98 n. 10.

45. *Science, Faith and Society*, pp. 66-67.

46. *Personal Knowledge*, pp. 201-202.

47. *Ibid.*, p. 321.

48. William H. Bossart, "Three Directions of Phenomenology," in *The Anatomy of Knowledge*, edited by Marjorie Grene (Amherst: University of Massachusetts Press, 1969), p. 276.

49. For instances of Polanyi's expression of the contribution of Gestalt psychology to the development of his theory, see *Science, Faith and Society*, pp. 11-12 and 24; *Personal Knowledge*, pp. 55-57; *The Study of Man*, pp. 28-29; and *The Tacit Dimension*, pp. 6-8.

50. For example, Marjorie Grene, following the lead of Whitehead, discusses the effect of Hume's phenomenalism coupled with Cartesian-Newtonian common-sense assumptions on space and time and points to the resulting paradox of raw data without any basis of interpretation facing a system with only accidental rationale for its success. See *The Knower and the Known*, pp. 96-98. A similar assessment is presented from the vantage point of Hobbes' materialism in her "Hobbes and the Modern Mind," in *The Anatomy of Knowledge*, pp. 1-28.

51. *The Tacit Dimension*, pp. 7-8, 13-15, and 95 n. 1 and 2. Recall also our earlier discussion of inarticulate intelligence. The point under consideration here is, in Polanyi's estimation, a particular instance of the tacit structure which pervades the entire realm of living beings in their orientation to their surroundings. For further empirical research upon which his thesis is based, see *Personal Knowledge*, pp. 71-76, 122-123 and *The Tacit Dimension*, pp. 42-46.

52. Polanyi derives this set of terms from anatomy. See *The Tacit Dimension*, pp. 10 and 13.

53. *The Tacit Dimension*, pp. 7 and 29.

54. *The Study of Man*, pp. 28-30.

55. It is helpful to clarify this point by recalling our earlier discussion of Polanyi's contention that absolutely explicit and objective knowledge is specious and that all instances of explicit knowledge are sustained only in relation to their tacit component. Thus when my focal knowledge, which is an achievement of my tacit knowing, leads me to assert "This is a typewriter," it is quite valid to consider the statement "explicit" in the normal sense of the word. But in so doing we must keep in mind that it is "explicit" because of the focal knowledge we have of it through out subsidiary reliance on the particulars which constitute it. Accordingly what was previously subsidiary (our joint integration of the keys, ribbon, characteristic shape, etc., and the use to which they are

put) may in their turn be focused upon and be made tempo-rarily "explicit," as would happen if we tried to explain to someone why we called that object a typewriter. For a further discussion of this point, see Edward Pols, "Polan-yi and the Problem of Metaphysical Knowledge," in *Intel-lect and Hope*, pp. 67-69.

56. Polanyi, however, is careful to note (in *The Tacit Dimen-sion* p. 15) that this does not explain how consciousness arises in man. "It merely applies the general principle that wherever some process in our body gives rise to consciousness in us, our tacit knowing of the process will make sense of it in terms of an experience to which we are attending."

57. In this expanded use of the term "indwelling," Polanyi is aware that he is modifying its usual meaning. Obviously his intention is not to say that the indwelling involved in our use of a tool or our reliance on a conceptual sys-tem is literally and precisely the same as the indwelling which describes our bodily existence. Rather, the ex-tended use of indwelling is to be taken "in a logical sense as affirming that the parts of the external world, when interiorized, function in the same way as our body functions when we attend from it to things outside." "Science and Man's Place in the Universe," in *Science as a Cultural Force*, edited by Harry Woolf (Baltimore: Johns Hopkins University Press, 1964), p. 63.

58. See *The Tacit Dimension*, pp. 14-15, 24-25, and 29.

59. See *The Study of Man*, pp. 82-83; "On the Modern Mind," 20; and "Faith and Reason," *Journal of Religion*, XLI (1961), 242-244.

60. See Lecture Three, "Understanding History," in *The Study of Man*.

61. *The Tacit Dimension*, pp. 16-17.

62. See Marjorie Grene, *The Knower and the Known*, Ch. 6, "Facts and Values," for a further discussion of this as-pect of Polanyi's thought.

63. *The Tacit Dimension*, pp. 78 and 87.

64. The metaphysical problem of our knowledge of "reality" will be discussed in the next chapter.

65. The broad outlines of Polanyi's theory (as were indicated above, pp. 47-49 and 51-52) were first presented in *Per-sonal Knowledge*, especially pp. 49-131 and briefly in *The Study of Man*, pp. 21-25 and 60-61. Here we shall indicate his more recent proposals which are expressed chiefly in "Sense-Giving and Sense-Reading," in *Knowing and Being*, pp. 181-207.

66. "Sense-Giving and Sense-Reading," pp. 184-185. See also

"The Logic of Tacit Inference," in *Knowing and Being*, pp. 146-147.

67. "Sense-Giving and Sense-Reading," pp. 185-187.

68. *Ibid.*, pp. 189-190.

69. *Ibid.*, pp. 190-191; "The Logic of Tacit Inference," p. 149; and "Tacit Knowing: Its Bearing on Some Problems of Philosophy," pp. 165-168.

70. "Tacit Knowing: Its Bearing on Some Problems of Philosophy," p. 170. See also Grene, *The Knower and the Known*, pp. 58-63 for a comparison of Polanyi's understanding with Aristotle's.

71. See "The Logic of Tacit Inference," pp. 145 and 157.

72. "Sense-Giving and Sense-Reading," p. 192.

73. Polanyi relies on Noam Chomsky--quoting directly from his *Aspects of the Theory of Syntax* (Cambridge: Massachusetts Institute of Technology Press, 1965), pp. 56-58--for the formulation of the problems involved. See "Sense-Giving and Sense-Reading," pp. 196, 204 and 207.

74. "Tacit Knowing: Its Bearing on Some Problems of Philosophy," pp. 170-171.

75. "The Unaccountable Element in Science," pp. 110-114.

76. The tacit reliance on a background, which may assume a variety of forms--including, as we shall see, linguistic and cultural backgrounds, functions in a manner similar to the "horizon" described by phenomenology, although within the context of personal knowledge it refers to an element involved in a dynamic process rather than simply a state of consciousness. See Helmut Kuhn, "Personal Knowledge and the Crisis of the Philosophical Tradition," in *Intellect and Hope*, p. 116.

77. This appraisal relies on Victor Preller's reinterpretation of the epistemology of Thomas Aquinas in light of the thought of Wilfred Sellars. Though Preller intends to clarify Thomas' meaning of intelligibility by means of this analysis, it is equally applicable to, or at least consistent with, Polanyi's understanding of language. See *Divine Science and the Science of God* (Princeton, N.J.: Princeton University Press, 1967), pp. 86-88.

78. See Marjorie Grene, *The Knower and the Known*, p. 145.

79. See above, pp. 66-68.

80. *Personal Knowledge*, p. 374; and also p. 363.

81. The discussion which follows is based on *The Study of Man*, pp. 86-89; see also pp. 76-77.

82. *The Tacit Dimension*, pp. 82-83.

83. *Personal Knowledge*, p. 404.

84. *The Tacit Dimension*, p. 91.

85. *Personal Knowledge*, p. 403.

86. "The Creative Imagination," 92.

87. "Knowing and Being," p. 133.

88. *The Tacit Dimension*, p. 87.

CHAPTER IV

THE LOGIC OF EMERGENCE

When Michael Polanyi began his inquiries into the mode of
human knowing, the particular issue which provoked his quest
was the controversy concerning the organization of science.
During the 1930's in England a movement was initiated to organize science according to some socially designed plan. Polanyi, along with some colleagues, opposed any such organization
of science and argued in favor of the traditional independence
of scientific inquiry. While engaged in this effort Polanyi
found that the supports for this position had eroded. While
the attempt to organize science according to some central plan
has since been abandoned in the West, the problem of articulating the foundations of a free scientific inquiry in search
of truth nevertheless remained. To this task Polanyi then
dedicated his efforts.

The first systematic exposition of his thought, expressed
in *Science, Faith and Society*, viewed science as a specialized
form of perception dependent on the consensus of the scientific
community. To the network of meanings, values, and methods
embodied in this scientific tradition the individual scientist
commits himself, and thus endowed he brings his perception to
bear on new possible conceptions of reality. Since science is
a sub-group within the entire cultural setting, the whole range
of human endeavors could be analyzed in this light. Polanyi
was thus led to the more adventurous undertaking of probing the
foundations of human thought in general.

The crucial problem at this stage of Polanyi's development
was the question concerning how we could affirm a body of knowledge which was not indubitably grounded. The previous chapter
attempted to outline Polanyi's response to this problem. Here

the argument was detailed in such a way as to show that the
performance of our acts of knowing was valid even though its
ultimate basis consisted in responsible judgment made with universal intent. By uncovering the dynamic process grounding our
thought Polanyi showed how our commitment to our systems of
thought could result in progressively more adequate representations of reality.

Since that time Polanyi has focused his attention on clarifying the structural elements of tacit knowing. The result of
this effort was that his reliance on the notion of commitment
as an explanation for the validity of our knowledge has been
reduced.[1] While this represents a development in his thought,
it is not a radical departure from his earlier insights, because the aspects of tacit knowing are the very elements which
implicitly grounded his original understanding of human knowledge.[2] At the same time the roots of tacit knowing may now be
recognized as necessarily grounded in that to which it refers.
By means of his analysis of the structure of tacit knowing,
therefore, Polanyi has been able to situate the reality of the
human knower within the panorama of a logic of evolutionary
emergence. In turn this structural development has enabled
Polanyi to establish more firmly the universal role of indwelling wherein our knowledge of reality is necessarily assumed.
For this reason we have postponed until now a delineation of
the ontological implications of personal knowledge. We shall
accordingly explicate the structure of tacit knowing from which
an understanding of our knowledge of reality will emerge. The
implications derived from this horizon will, finally, provide
the outlines of a foundational theology for accrediting the
meaning and significance of religious faith.

A. *The Structure of Tacit Knowing*

1. The functional structure of tacit knowing

A basic logical relation operates to constitute and sustain all our acts of knowledge. This underlying relationship,
which combines two kinds of knowing, has already been expressed
in several ways. In an act of comprehension, we rely on a subsidiary awareness of the particulars of an entity in order that

we may be focally aware of the whole they constitute. Or we may say that we are aware of the distal term of tacit knowing through our reliance on the proximal. Finally this relationship has been described as attending from the particulars to the whole. This is the functional structure of tacit knowing.[3] Our acts of tacit knowing function to direct us to a coherent understanding of reality. We are guided from the proximal, subsidiarly held interiorized particulars to their integration in a distal, focally known, coherent whole.[4]

An important feature of this functional structure of tacit knowing is the recognition that its achievement is an integration, not a deduction. The comprehension of an object by means of a reliance on its particulars cannot be formally explained. The inference is non-explicit or tacit. By means of this understanding of tacit integration Polanyi has uncovered the process which enables him to explain the varied dimensions of our experience ranging from simple perception to the induction leading to scientific discovery.[5]

This integrative capacity of tacit knowing described by its functional structure may be clarified by recalling the irreversibility of such an achievement. In an explicit form of inference, we may retrace our steps. This does not hold, however, in the case of a tacit integration. The return to the original state before the integration (sometimes an impossibility in itself) destroys the comprehension which had been attained.[6] A simple illustration of this phenomenon adduced by Polanyi is the example of stereo-pictures viewed through the machine which combines the two distinct pictures into a three-dimensional perspective. We cannot, upon removal of the pictures from the viewer, identify explicitly how we integrated the pictures, nor can we see the coherent picture at all. The particulars no longer function as clues to a comprehensive whole and the logical disintegration reduces them to a set of more or less meaningless fragments.

A final consideration on the functional structure of tacit knowing is a cautionary note. Polanyi has often found it necessary to stress the fact that our subsidiary awareness is not to be equated with an unconscious, pre-conscious, or subliminal awareness, nor with the notion of the fringe of awareness.[7]

The degree of consciousness or the lack of it is not the defin-
ing characteristic of subsidiary knowledge; rather it is the
function it fulfills. That which is subsidiarily known may
have any degree of consciousness, provided it serves as a clue
to our focal awareness.

2. The phenomenal aspect of tacit knowing

From the basic structure of tacit knowing, three further
aspects may now be discerned. The first of these concerns the
shape or appearance the particulars assume upon being tacitly
integrated.

In general the appearance of the particulars assumes a new
shape as a result of our awareness of them in the whole which
they constitute. We are aware of the proximal term of tacit
knowing in its appearance as the distal term. The integration
of the particulars into a coherent fashion brings about our
awareness of a quality which is not apparent in the dismembered
particulars. This is the phenomenal aspect of tacit knowing.[8]

The phenomenal aspect of tacit knowing may be illustrated
in the case of our recognition of a physiognomy. We are aware
of the features which constitute a physiognomy in terms of our
awareness of the physiognomy itself. Similarly, when we perform a skillful action, we are aware of the sensations and
muscular dexterity in terms of the operations to which our attention is directed. The phenomenal aspect thus points to that
element of the functional relation of our tacit knowledge whereby we are aware of that from which we are attenting to another
dimension in the appearance of that reality.

This understanding of the phenomenal aspect of tacit knowing provides an explanation of our ability to interpret the
same set of particulars in different ways. A particular set
of "data" can often be viewed from different backgrounds which
may be simply alternative ways of viewing the phenomenon in
question or may be progressively more penetrating. The familiar figures of Gestalt psychology illustrate quite clearly that
the same set of particulars can be seen alternatively as different phenomena depending on how these particulars are tacitly integrated. Where it is a question of a more penetrating
perception, however, much depends on the attentiveness, imagi-

nativeness, and insightfulness brought to the situation by the knower. Thus one person may walk through the woods and see nothing but trees, rocks, and clods of dirt, while another person, a trained naturalist for example, may see specific species of oaks, elms, conifers, and even animals well camouflaged by the environment. Similarly two individuals who are engaged in the creative effort of probing the frontiers of thought described by their horizons held in common, may approach a particular set of circumstances or "data" in different ways. The result will be that the elements they have discovered will appear to them in different ways. Their reliance on the particulars and their tacit integration of them are performed in a different manner so that they seem to be describing contradictory phenomena. Gradually one of these perceptions will come to be accepted as more adequately integrating the particulars in question according to the criteria now imposed by the enlarged framework or horizon. The controversy between Priestly and Lavoisier is a case in point.[9]

An important feature of the phenomenal aspect of tacit knowing consists in the recognition that the particulars which are tacitly integrated are relied upon in order to focus on a quality not apparent in the particulars themselves. This shows that the ability to perceive certain phenomena requires a prior preparation or at least an openness on the part of the knower. In the illustration of the naturalist, we see that his heightened awareness, due to a long period of training and the personal effort of incorporating a particular horizon of his cultural heritage, enables him to rely on certain particulars and to grasp a quality of their integrated appearance in a manner not appreciated by one whose awareness was not so trained. Furthermore, since the phenomenal aspect is an outcome of the functional structure of tacit knowing, it follows that an analysis which would examine the constituent parts of the phenomenon in question would be destructive for the comprehension of the phenomenon, at least while the analysis was taking place. The result of this understanding is to provide a clue for reinstating the validity of "secondary" qualities[10] and ultimately for validating the possibility of religious knowledge.

3. The semantic aspect of tacit knowing

The relationship between the two terms of tacit knowing assumes further significance which is grounded on the combination of the functional and phenomenal aspects of tacit knowing. When we focally attend to a phenomenon, it is the meaning of the particulars to which we are attending; the particulars mean that phenomenon. Or we may say that the appearance of that to which we are attending is derived from the meaning of the particulars. This reliance on the particulars to focus on their joint meaning is the semantic aspect of tacit knowing.[11]

An important characteristic of this semantic aspect is that meaning is displaced from ourselves. We attend from our tacit knowledge of the proximal term to our focal knowledge of the distal term. We tacitly know the interiorized particulars through the meaning they attain when this meaning refers to a coherent entity. This is precisely the meaning of the traditional notion of "the intelligibility of being."[12] All our knowledge possesses this directedness or intentionality. This is due to its being grounded in our bodily indwelling. Even though the semantic aspect of our tacit knowledge, with its from-to or intentional structure, implies that our knowledge of reality cannot be accounted for or justified by explicit procedures, such knowledge does not rest on pure caprice. Human thought is dependent on the particulars it embodies.[13] Through the integration of these particulars, the reality which they comprise is endowed with meaning.

4. The ontological aspect of tacit knowing

The structure of tacit knowing explains the dynamic elements of the fundamental, a-critical processes which ground every explicit affirmation. Our dwelling in the world, rooted in our bodily existence, is presupposed in every claim we make. The subsidiary elements, which represent the particulars of an entity and which we incorporate to form an integral whole which appears to us under a particular framework and is thus endowed with meaning, lead us beyond ourselves to the comprehension of something *real*. In other words, the proximal term of our tacit knowing operates as a token with a bearing on

reality which is expressed in our assertions as the distal term.
Implied in every act of tacit knowing is a claim that what is
known is real. This is the ontological aspect of tacit knowing.[14]

The plausibility of this claim rests on the recognition
that, as William Poteat puts it, "the subjunctive mood is, ontologically, parasitical upon a primordial indicative."[15] All
of our knowledge, whether it concerns statements of fact, theoretical formulations, performances of a skill, or the heuristic probings of the creative imagination, unfolds within a context tacitly held by a person--a context including his being in
the world through his bodily existence. Whenever we are in the
act of making a judgment, its propositional form can be evaluated only within the context of our indwelling as the concomitant ground of our affirmation having a bearing on reality.
Only as a consequence of this indicative mood can the proposi-
tion be evaluated noncomitally or subjunctively.[16]

Our tacit knowledge implies a fundamental and, during its
performance, an indubitable claim that what it asserts has a
bearing on reality. This claim, even though never wholly in-
defeasible, holds that the *act* of tacit knowing results in an
understanding of an aspect of reality.[17] The validity of the
propositional form of this act is an inquiry of another
order: it is a question of its truth. Insofar as the propo-
sition which conveys the meaning of our affirmation is held to
be true, there is the further implication that the aspect of
reality it expresses may, in turn, lead to new revelations of
that reality in ways as yet unknown and perhaps still unthinkable. Our attention must now move to an explication of this
understanding of reality.

B. *The Meaning of Reality*

Our investigations thus far have uncovered an understanding of the fundamental structure of all human knowing. Included in this structure is a primordial reference to the real
which is inherent in the act of affirmation. Through our personal indwelling we tacitly rely on our bodily processes which
interiorize aspects of reality and integrate them into a focal
comprehension. We expand our personal base into the world

through our linguistic and historical indwelling by assimilating further sets of particulars expressed in conceptual and cultural forms in order to understand a universe composed of coherent entities.

The significance of this tacit reference to the real in every act of affirmation can be illustrated in several ways. The scientist pursuing a problem relies on an existing body of knowledge which he has interiorized to guide himself in perceiving aspects of reality which, because he regards them to be real, function as clues or indicators to an ever more diverse range of manifestations.[18] Because of this reference to the real, his anticipated discovery will be fully determined, even though he has at present only a vague intimation or a tacit foreknowledge of what it will be.

The situation is similar, but of a more complex character, when one person recognizes an entity which another person is doing, such as an effort at communication, the performance of a skill, or playing a game of chess. Intrinsic to an understanding of chess, for example, is an appreciation of that which accounts for the coherence of the game: a person working out a strategy according to a set of formal rules. Such a recognition is a necessary precondition for understanding any sort of coordinated performance. We do not, as some would have it, infer the reality of "another mind" from its external workings; normally we do not observe these workings in themselves at all. Rather our knowledge of other persons is like the process of scientific inquiry where we rely on clues, many of which are unspecifiable during the act of knowing, to comprehend the reality to which they refer.[19]

A final illustration for our understanding the significance of the tacit reference to reality in our affirmations is our recognition of a concrete object. As we have already seen in the previous chapter, our comprehension of solid, concrete entities manifests the same qualities as the act which constitutes our knowledge of a scientific theory or another mind. We know an entity, such as a cobblestone, by relying on a subsidiary awareness of its particulars in order to be aware of it focally and affirm its reality in a judgment. We do not, in other words, simply "look out there" and see things. It is

our intentional activity, guided by our reliance on a conceptual framework tacitly known and our integration of the particulars of the entity in light of this framework which enables
us to "see" such things as cobblestones and affirm their reality.

The structural similarities on the part of the knower involved in affirming a cobblestone, a theory, or a person to be
real lead to a recognition of the difference between the reality of a stone in comparison with a theory or a person. A
scientist regards a theory as expressing a real feature of nature. He considers it real because he expects the laws embodied
in it to reveal themselves indeterminately in the future. Persons likewise manifest this dimension of an inexhaustible range
of future self-revelations. In this sense they are more profoundly real than cobblestones. This ability of something to
manifest itself indefinitely is, for Polanyi, a criterion of
its being real; and the degree to which it possesses this ability is a manifestation of its profundity. Based upon these
observations, Polanyi concludes:

> This capacity of a thing to reveal itself in un-
> expected ways in the future I attribute to the fact
> that the thing observed is an aspect of reality,
> possessing a significance that is not exhausted by
> our conception of any single aspect of it. To
> trust that a thing we know is real is, in this
> sense, to feel that it has the independence and
> power for manifesting itself in yet unthought of
> ways in the future. I shall say, accordingly,
> that minds and problems possess a deeper reality
> than cobblestones, although cobblestones are ad-
> mittedly more real in the sense of being *tangible*.
> And since I regard the significance of a thing as
> more important than its tangibility, I shall say
> that minds and problems are more real than cobble-
> stones.[20]

This understanding of reality, to which Polanyi often refers in
his later writings as a definition of reality,[21] introduces in
a preliminary fashion a criterion for uncovering the significance of the ontological aspect of all acts of tacit knowing.

The primary significance of this criterion consists in its
comparative use which is in turn grounded in the recognition of
the structure of tacit knowing. We know things by comprehending them, and this comprehension has the same structure as the
entity which is its object. Thus the skillful performance of a

game of chess by a master is a reality whose structure is similar to our act of comprehending it. The existence of knowledge and the person who manifests it have ontological implications. They are real things and in light of their indeterminate implications more real than cobblestones. This recognition leads Polanyi to assert that "it seems plausible then to assume in all other instances of tacit knowing the correspondence between the structure of comprehension and the structure of the comprehensive entity which is its object."[22]

There are, admittedly, several difficulties involved in this proposal. One might object that Polanyi is using existence as a predicate--a highly suspect procedure since the time of Kant. Or it might be pointed out, that while *persons* may be understood in some sense to be more real than cobblestones, it it another matter when Polanyi wishes to assert that our knowledge of a good problem is more real than a physical object. In order to discuss such objections intelligently, however, we must first delineate what is meant by this correspondence in structure between the knower and the thing known and the degree of reality attributed to each. This ultimately requires an understanding of man.

C. The Meaning of Man

1. Levels of reality

In the preceding section Polanyi's criterion for understanding reality, as that which can manifest itself indefinitely in the future, suggested a comparative use whereby persons were acknowledged to be more real than simple physical objects. It was stated further that the basis upon which a greater degree of reality was attributed to man was the assumption of a correspondence in the structure of knowing with the thing known. Implicit in these observations is the traditional notion of a hierarchy of being or levels of reality. In order to justify this understanding of a person as being more real than a simply physical entity we must provide an explanation of the levels of reality which can account for such a hierarchy in a consistent and meaningful fashion.

We may begin by recalling that in an act of tacit knowing

an integration of the particulars of an entity is achieved so
that we may focally attend to the entity. If we destroy this
integration by attending to the particulars in themselves, we
no longer comprehend focally the entity which they constitute.
Insofar as there is a counterpart to this in the structure of
comprehensive entities, we should expect a set of principles
governing the particulars of the entity for their manner of
operation but that these principles would not account for their
organization in such a way that they could be understood to
constitute the entity itself. In other words, the two terms
of tacit knowing would correspond to two distinct levels of
reality in the comprehensive entity, with the upper level dependent on the lower but inexplicable in terms of the principles
which constitute this lower level.

This general scheme can now be exemplified by a consideration of the structure of an entity from the realm of inanimate
nature which will exhibit two distinct levels of reality. To
do this we will analyze the structure of a machine, an example
frequently used by Polanyi.[23]

In physics, researchers often place restrictions on the
workings of nature in order to set up an experimental situation. These useful restrictions are referred to as an imposi-
tion of *boundary conditions* on physical and chemical laws.[24]
Such boundary conditions are extraneous to the process which
they are delimiting. As an example, Polanyi points to Galileo's
experiments deriving the laws of mechanics, in which he rolled
spheres down a slope. The angle of the slope was a condition
set by Galileo, extraneous as such to the laws he uncovered by
subjecting the spheres to this condition.[25] A machine can now
be seen to impose a set of operational principles on the boundary conditions left open by inanimate nature, but with a different purpose. Now they are imposed not to observe an instance
of a physical law, but to achieve some aim defined by the operational principles of the machine itself. In this case the boundary conditions left indeterminate by the laws of nature expressed in physics and chemistry are controlled by an extraneous set of operational principles which describe the function
of the machine. Since the principles which describe the operation of the machine control the boundary conditions of physical

laws, they can in no way be accounted for by these physical
laws. Such control exercised by the operational principles of
a higher level of a comprehensive entity on the particulars of
a lower level which are left open by their boundary conditions
Polanyi terms the *principle of marginal control.*[26]

A comprehensive entity, such as a machine, is thus subject
to a dual control.[27] The operational principles describing the
purpose of the machine artificially shape the material components of the machine. They do not abrogate the laws of physics
or chemistry, but govern their boundary conditions. Consequently, the principles of both levels operate jointly. The laws of
physics and chemistry will continue to operate, even though the
marginal control exercised by the machine's operational principles breaks down. A machine is thus liable to failure in a
way physical and chemical laws are not because it controls the
boundary conditions of material whose own principles (i.e.,
physical and chemical laws) operate irrespective of this marginal control exercised by the machine's operational principles.[28]

The distinctive level of the operational principles which
define a machine can be further specified when the class of the
machine is considered. If, for example, a steam engine were to
be described by physics and chemistry, the laws of thermodynamics could be used to characterize the atomic topography of the
machine. But they do not define a steam engine: only engineering, which is a distinct science dealing with the operational principles of engines, can specify how a machine relies
on the boundary conditions to use the laws of thermodynamics.
The class of a machine cannot be identified, in other words, by
an appeal to a set of physical or chemical laws.[29] Only the
recognition of a distinctive level in the machine can account
for its classification among all other machines.

The conclusion to which these considerations on the structure of machines lead us is that all more or less permanent
comprehensive entities exhibit this same hierarchic relationship between their constitutive levels functioning according
to the principle of marginal control. This dual relationship
is often comprised of several interconnected hierarchical levels, where each level operates according to its own principles
and each in their turn forms a set of boundary conditions upon

which the succeeding level builds by the marginal control it
exercises over the next lower level. Human speech is a clear
illustration of such an expanded sequence of levels. Sounds,
words, grammar, style, and purpose function in this way to compose a reality called communication. It follows that an adequate comprehension of an entity can be achieved only by tacitly integrating the diverse levels which constitute it, so that
its distinct and highest level, which tells us what it is, may
become the focus of our attention.

In terms of Polanyi's understanding of reality, these reflections mean that reality itself is composed of diverse, interdependent levels.

> In a hierarchic sequence of comprehensive levels
> each higher level is related to the levels below
> it in the same way as the operations of a machine
> are related to the particulars obeying the laws of
> physics. You cannot explain the operations of an
> upper level in terms of the particulars on which
> its operations rely. Each higher level of inte-
> gration represents, in this sense, a higher level
> of existence, not accountable by the levels below
> it.[30]

This "higher level of existence" attributed to the integrating
level of a comprehensive entity provides a preliminary understanding of Polanyi's criterion of reality. Machines are more
real than their physical components insofar as they cannot be
explained by a simple appeal to these constituent elements:
machines reveal, through their harnessing of the boundary conditions of inanimate nature, possibilities not contained in
nature as such, even though they are thoroughly dependent on
the principles of nature. To this extent machines manifest in
a very elementary way consequences unforeseen by physics and
chemistry. Furthermore Polanyi's critique of the reductivist
program of Laplace now is given an ontological as well as a
logical foundation. Things that are less tangible, such as the
operational principles of a machine, are more real, because
they represent a higher level of existence than the obviously
tangible components which these operational principles control.

These reflections would seem to hold equally for an understanding of life. There is, however, a fundamental difference
between a machine and a living thing which necessitates further
clarifications before such a judgment may be validly made.

Since machines are human artifacts and are extraneously used
to shape boundary conditions of inanimate nature, they cannot
be produced spontaneously by nature itself. But the morphological structures of living things are not so produced. Is it
possible that such structures grow to maturity simply because
of the operations of physical-chemical laws? Polanyi's answer
is negative, and we must now turn to an exposition of his reasons for this conclusion.

2. The emergence of life

Any discussion on the irreducibility of life to physical
and chemical laws must first clarify the ambiguity present in
the predominant view of biologists which assumes that a mechanistic explanation of life is virtually equivalent to its explanation by the laws of inanimate nature.[31] This assumption
is held even by that minority group of biologists who wish to
argue that not *all* properties of life can be understood through
a mechanistic model and therefore postulate organismic processes to account for living functions. As a result of Polanyi's
analysis of the structure of a machine in relation to its
physical components, this claim is clearly mistaken. The ambiguity of the claim can then be clarified by recognizing that
much can be learned from the interpretation of many biological
functions as machine-like. The point being made here is that,
while a machine-like explanation of an organ adds to our understanding of the biotic processes of the organism, it may not be
construed as explaining the living thing by means of physical
and chemical laws.

This may be seen very briefly by recalling that physics
and chemistry are meaningful only within a set of boundary conditions which form a framework for understanding the operation
of their laws and which are not derived from these laws. Accordingly, whenever biophysicists and biochemists attempt to
explain biotic processes, they are always concerned with these
processes only insofar as they are relevant to an existing organism. Thus biological principles form the boundary conditions
under which such research is conducted. The laws of physics and
chemistry are now studied within this framework of dual control,
so that only those chemical and physical aspects which relate to

the living entity are considered to be part of the science. In other words, the principle of marginal control, with the biotic processes forming the upper level, now determines the conditions under which physical and chemical properties are studied. Biophysics and biochemistry simply elucidate as thoroughly as possible the physical and chemical principles on which the living thing relies and which its own operational principles control.[32]

In light of these clarifications, we may now rephrase our original question on the development of an organism in this way: Can the constitutive properties of a developing organism shape their own boundary conditions without these properties themselves becoming subject to a set of extraneous boundaries such as organismic principles? An adequate treatment of this problem requires an examination of the claims made by Crick for DNA. Polanyi's contention is that the control of morphogenesis by DNA is similar to the control of an engineer in the design of a machine. For our purposes it will suffice simply to summarize the general outline of his argument.[33]

We may begin by assuming the prevailing view, espoused by Crick, that DNA determines entirely the growth of the organism. We are then faced with an overwhelming redundancy. If, as both Watson and Crick maintain, DNA transmits a code or a blueprint, it must function as a boundary condition on its chemical makeup. Otherwise its chemical properties are the effective source for the pattern of development, and DNA as such is rendered superfluous. This is precisely the case, of course, in the structural bonding of an ordinary chemical molecule. But insofar as DNA is understood to control the genetic development of an organism by transmitting a code, it cannot be understood to achieve this by the exclusive means of its chemical properties. Rather, it must be understood to be effecting a set of boundary conditions on these properties.

In the development of the living organism, then, DNA forms part of the morphological structure of the organism and thus is irreducible to physics and chemistry. It transmits to the cell a quantity of information not found in physics or chemistry (though dependent on their operation), and thus it transcends physical and chemical laws. The growth of an organism results in a configuration of particles which is highly improbable and in no way shaped by the principles of physics and chemistry. This shaping by DNA is thus analogous to the shaping of a machine by an engineer.

Furthermore, DNA cannot be understood as fixing its own boundary conditions. Because of the information brought to the organism within the morphological framework, the shaping of the organism by DNA is more than a stabilization of an almost infinite number of possible configurations. Such shaping "achieves control of the boundaries by imprinting a significant pattern on the boundaries of the system. Or, to use information language, we may say that it puts the system under the control of a non-physical-chemical principle by *a profoundly informative intervention*."[34] As a result of the control exercised by DNA on physical and chemical properties, a higher principle operates by controlling the entire morphological development. This higher level then is not simply produced by DNA, for it is not reducible to it. "It appears," according to Polanyi, "that DNA *evokes* the ontogenesis of higher levels, rather than *determining* these levels."[35]

Such evocations may be likened to the integration of particulars by tacit knowing, especially when seen in light of the paradigm case of problem solving. A poet, for example, possesses a tacit intimation of a potential coherence of disparate words, feelings, and insights which he proceeds to integrate in his work by establishing a new comprehensive entity which expresses this coherence. Thus emerges a new poem.

Before we continue this exposition of Polanyi's argument, we shall pause for a moment to clarify two points concerning the distinction between biotic levels and the level of inanimate nature. The first clarification concerns a precision on the meaning of the irreducibility of the former to the latter. The irreducibility intended cannot be equated simply with a recognition that a comprehensive system displays features not observable in its disparate particulars.[36] Holistic systems, such as the spherical shape of planets and the ordered aggregates that make up crystals, are to be found in physics and chemistry. Since they may be reducible to physical and chemical laws as in the above examples, the comprehensiveness of systems which display qualities not immediately discernible in their components is not a sufficient criterion in itself for recognizing the distinctiveness of living beings.

The second clarification concerns the admission of a kind of continuity between living things and inanimate nature. This does not negate the irreducibility of life to nature. Rather it points to the fact that the difference between a highly complex chemical structure and a very simple cell may not be clearly identifiable. The control of the living organism over its boundary conditions may be minimal. "The fact that the effect of a higher principle over a system of dual control can have any value down to zero may allow us to conceive a continuous emergence of irreducible principles within the origin of life."[37] The systems of dual control, in other words, must be conceived as ranging over a wide spectrum down to that point where the upper level disappears totally and the lower level takes over complete control of the particulars which formerly constituted the living entity.

Keeping these considerations in mind, we may now return to the major focus of Polanyi's argument. Inanimate nature, the workings of which are defined by physical and chemical laws, operates infallibly. It cannot fail because it does not achieve anything. As soon as a living being enters the picture, however, all this is changed. Intrinsic to a living being is some purpose which it may or may not achieve. The only reasonable conclusion, which may be drawn from this in light of Polanyi's analysis, is that a set of operational principles, not present in nature, comes into being when life arises.

Furthermore the hierarchic structure commonly recognized in the forms of life requires the admission of higher levels of emergence. Since the higher levels of life, such as the instinctive, control lower levels, such as the muscular, the boundary conditions of these lower levels must be left open and cannot be understood to produce the higher levels. "Thus the logical structure of the hierarchy implies that a higher level can come into existence only through a process not manifest in the lower level, a process which thus qualifies as an emergence."[38]

This emergence is one which entails the creation of new comprehensive entities and which requires an expanded framework for understanding the significance of evolution.[39] The crucial problem in facing any evolutionary theory is the very fact of the emergence of life and the rise of higher forms of life, including man, from lower forms. As we had pointed out earlier, however, the predominant scientific view of evolution employs as its chief explanatory tools natural selection and chance or random statistical variations of population groups due to external events. This has resulted in diverting the focus of attention from the fundamental question of how any single individual of a species had come into existence to the quite distinct problem of the origin of species. Consequently the possibility of fundamental innovations achieved by living things --even if in conjunction with environmental assistance--leading to new forms of biotic existence cannot be acknowledged by the prevailing scientific paradigm. Once this distinction[40] is recognized, however, the evolutionary emergence of novel forms of life may be seen to be both a real achievement and a gradual ascent with a hierarchy of real levels.

In addition to the distinct ontological levels which operate in all biotic forms of existence, the conception of evolution as emergence also recognizes the gradual and, at times, almost imperceptible process which produces fundamental innovations.[41] In the hierarchic structure outlined so far, the higher level of an individual organism controls the boundary conditions left open by the lower. Even though the upper level represents a distinct ontological level of existence, not reducible to the lower, it nevertheless relies on the workings of the operational principles of the lower level and channels them by controlling their boundary conditions, but it does not abrogate them. As a result, every new consolidation in the evolutionary ascent of life brings with itself an increasing possibility of failure. In short, the emergence of greater capabilities is always accompanied by increased liabilities.

A necessary concomitant to this recognition of increasing levels of achievement accompanied by their liabilities is the acknowledgment of a center of individuality for each living organism. On relatively low levels of emergence, where a consolidation of capabilities and liabilities is weakly controlled by a set of higher operational principles, this center of individuality will not necessarily be immediately evident. But its manifestations become more clearly perceptible as we pass from vegitative life to animal behavior. In other words, whenever we recognize an individual living thing at any level of existence, we tacitly acknowledge that it achieves some degree of success or failure. At least two profound consequences follow from this.

First, since our identification of the existence of an individual includes the attribution to it of some degree of success or failure, this implies that the center of individuality of any living being at any level of existence is real.[42] In order to comprehend it, we focus our attention on the coherence that is its higher level by subsidiarily integrating the particulars of its lower levels. And because we critically appraise its achievements and judge it to be real, we furthermore expect it to reveal more of itself indefinitely in future manifestations.

This implies, secondly, that we must dwell in a framework or horizon capable of dealing with life in order to know a living thing. A refusal to enter into such a biotic framework, if it could be pushed to its theoretical limits, would result in an instance of alienation which would preclude any knowledge of life by rendering all our common observations of living beings meaningless.[43] Normally this is not done, and probably cannot be done, in practice, because a very intimate form of shared indwelling is necessary for the recognition of life. Many modern biologists, who attempt to follow the ideal of the physical sciences, would perhaps feel uneasy with this contention, since it requires the admission of a grasp of a reality over and above the physical components of the animal. Yet this is precisely how we come to know the reality of living things. Polanyi's argument for the irreducibility of life to its physical components, including his elaboration of distinct ontological levels operating in all organic life, provides a substantial foundation for this everyday experience. And the theory of tacit knowing, whereby we incorporate the particulars of an object in order to integrate them and focus on their coherence, can be applied directly to the recognition of life: "The particulars of living beings are known as such by attending *from* them to their joint meaning which is the life of the organism."[44] The center of the animal's individuality is known and judged--at least tacitly--to be real, just as the more tangible components of its body.

In this sense, all our knowledge of life is convivial.[45] We know a living thing by dwelling in its potentialities and recognizing its liabilities, by appreciating its activities, and by understanding the meaningful way in which these activities are achieved. Only when we are willing to accept this higher form of indwelling can the center of the individual thing be accredited as real. Such conviviality, when it reaches the level of man, is transformed from a simple knowledge of life to the encounter of another person.

3. The emergence of thought

The panorama disclosed so far through this presentation of Polanyi's thought points to a confluence of evolution conceived as emergence with the tacit powers of man. After a preliminary indication of the contradictions and difficulties inherent in a strictly objectivist view of human knowledge, we proceeded to introduce Polanyi's conception of tacit knowing as an alternative which would overcome these difficulties by proposing a systematic framework to describe and explain more adequately the processes involved in the human mode of knowing. Tacit knowing was then seen to be an act of comprehension achieved by integrating particulars into their coherent meaning. Through an analysis of our own acts of cognition and a brief look at other human actions, we next saw that the entities being comprehended were similar in structure to the act of comprehension itself. The critical element of this insight consisted in the recognition that the relationship of a comprehensive entity to its constitutive elements is determined by the marginal control of the higher level of the reality over the boundary conditions left open by its lower level. This structural relationship then opened to view a stratified and hierarchical series of levels of reality, including all living things. From within this framework, finally, we were able to understand emergence as the action producing innovations leading toward higher levels of existence both by allowing individuals to develop and species to evolve.[46]

In this broadened perspective emergence functions as a general conception which accounts for creative advances on all biotic levels. As the achievements produced by emergence gradually rise to the higher levels of biotic existence, the tacit powers we first encountered begin to become discernible. Finally at the highest level of emergence, the specific form which emergence assumes is the human mode of knowing described by tacit knowledge. It is thus in this comprehensive setting that the process of emergence is transformed to tacit knowing in man. We meet again man, who creates new meanings out of his experience with reality by incorporating subsidiary elements in innovative ways so that he may comprehend them ever more adequately.

The problem in need of clarification now is twofold. First, we must be able to explain how man is a real emergence. This means primarily that the center of individuality of a human being must be shown to be a reality not totally accounted for by the lower levels which also make up human existence. Or, to use more traditional categories, the mind-body problem must be examined in such a way that we are not encumbered by the liabilities of an extraneous entity, called the "mind," which is somehow "in" the body. Yet at the same time, if man is an emergence, as Polanyi claims, then some systematic relationship must be offered which will satisfactorily explain the specifically human powers of thought. The basis for this explanation has already been indicated, though its specific application to man must still be demonstrated. Secondly, the significance of this for understanding man must be examined. If knowing is a real achievement, then what man is and may become will have a profound effect on how and what man might know.

We may begin by considering our "knowledge of other minds," as the problem is sometimes expressed. The act by which we know another person is the same as that by which we know life. By relying on a set of clues which constitute the external workings of another person's mind and tacitly integrating them, we recognize the person who performs them. We dwell in the external manifestations of the workings of another person in order to integrate their meaning into a focal whole which is the

center of individuality of the person. We do not, in other
words, observe the workings of another mind in themselves, and
then by a process of inference impute to these actions a mind.
*"We experience a man's mind as the joint meaning of his actions
by dwelling in his actions from outside."*[47] What Polanyi is
claiming is that any entity which is composed of different levels of reality can only be recognized adequately by acknowledging its most comprehensive elements which form its highest level.[48] This is routinely done whenever we recognize a friend.

An objection to this explanation that may be raised at
this point is articulated most forcefully by some linguistic
philosophers and behaviorist psychologists. A behaviorist, for
example, contends that all activity usually considered "mental"
can be fully explained--at least in principle--through an objective description of the overt behavior of the individual,
which would include, in addition to the conditioning of external events, the neurophysiological mechanisms of the brain. As
we had indicated earlier, however, this can only work by means
of a subtle pseudo-substitution. The behaviorist program could
work only if the particular overt action could be known focally and at the same time known as a human action. But this is
not possible. We can know a particular action as a human action only if it functions as a clue which we tacitly integrate
into a coherence which is the mind of the person performing the
action.[49]

From a different perspective Gilbert Ryle argues, in *The
Concept of Mind*, that body and mind are not two separate things
as though we could infer the existence of minds by observing
overt human behavior. With this Polanyi is, of course, in complete agreement. But because Ryle formulates the problem from
a completely objectivist framework, he can only conclude that
there is no such thing as mind and that our observations are
simply following the workings of another human being.[50]

While Polanyi rejects the conclusions to which behaviorists and many linguistic philosophers are led, he is generally
sympathetic to the thrust of their arguments insofar as they
point to the fallacies of a simplistic dualism. Unfortunately,
because they have operated out of objectivist presuppositions,
it appeared as though the only alternatives consisted in the

dichtomomy of a mind-body dualism or a one-dimensional ontology of materialism. Polanyi's theory of tacit knowing and the hierarchical stratification of reality through succeeding levels of marginal control attempt to break this spell.[51]

The significance of our knowledge of another person can now be further expanded with a view to clarifying his understanding of the distinct reality of the human person through a consideration of the case of visual perception. According to the theory of tacit knowing the impact of light beams on our eyes generates responses by our ocular muscles, retina, and the complex network of our brain cells, including such things as our memories of past experiences and linguistic frameworks. All of these responses serve as subsidiary elements which we tacitly integrate into a focal whole which is the object of our sight. In other words our conscious dealings with the world around us always rely subsidiarily on our bodies. Two distinct levels of awarness are operating together whenever we see something. A conscious act of perception therefore includes both the focal point, which is its object, and its subsidiary roots, which are comprised of the bodily responses to the elements constituting the object.

This analysis brings out the relationship of the mind and body from the vantage point of human consciousness. In order to express this relationship between the levels of consciousness briefly, Polanyi uses the term "from-to" experience.[52] We attend *from* the experience of the subsidiaries *to* their comprehensive feature. Thus we are not only conscious *of* things, but also conscious *from* subsidiaries, which includes our incorporation of the particulars of the comprehensive entity and, of course, their impact on our bodies. This means that a mind is a from-to experience, while the subsidiaries of this experience, if viewed focally, would be perceived as bodily mechanisms.

Before this understanding of the mind-body relationship is carried further, it will be helpful to recall a few points from the description of tacit knowing outlined earlier so that some difficulties which may present themselves here can be resolved.[53] First, we must admit that there is a radical transformation of the sensory qualities we experience from the particular colors, shapes, motion, and situation of a thing to the internal bodily

responses to which they correspond. This type of transformation, however, is common in human knowing, particularly in the
sounds of words we use and rely on to convey their explicit
meaning. Next, the displacement of meaning to the external object as the distal term of tacit knowing will not appear problematic as soon as we recall what was already discussed when we
analyzed our use of tools. And finally the claim that we are
subsidiarily aware of bodily events, including the neural
traces of the cortex, means that these events function by contributing to our awareness of a focal object through our reliance on them. It is by their functional relationship, not our
focal awareness, that we are tacitly aware of them.

This last point is important for understanding the function of human consciousness in knowing. By acknowledging it,
we admit that our awareness of objects includes even the integration of the cortical traces of the brain which we bring
to bear in our consciousness of them. In Polanyi's estimation
this analysis solves an experimental problem by accounting for
the unity of consciousness that we experience, even though
there is no anatomical point in the brain which could unify the
cortical traces.[54]

The relationship of body and mind may thus be seen as an
instance of the relationship described by subsidiary and focal
awareness.[55] In the process of perception we attend from a
set of subsidiary clues to the joint meaning they represent.
If a neurophysiologist were to describe thoroughly the bodily
processes which were operating while a subject was viewing an
object, he would be focusing on that which the subject was attending from. Seeing an object is quite different from seeing
the mechanism by which someone sees it. The subject alone can
experience the integration of the subsidiaries. The neurophysiologist, on the other hand, can only look at the bodily
responses of the subject. The distinct contents of these two
experiences are partially responsible for the attraction of a
Cartesian dualism.[56] From Polanyi's perspective, however, such
"dualism" results from our ability to shift the focus of our
attention from that to which our bodily mechanisms refer to
those mechanisms themselves.[57]

It would be facile to conclude from this, however, that

mind and body are simply two aspects of the same thing. Such a
parallelism would not account for both of the experiences described above. Furthermore, it would leave unexplained the
personal experience of the unity of consciousness and our ability to integrate our bodily processes. Polanyi points this out
by asserting that

> . . .the bearing by which we understand both the
> input and the output of a neurological process must
> be established by ourselves, by our interpretation
> of the behavioral signs of this input and output.
> *The neural functions supply these signs, but they
> do not supply their interpretation.* Since this
> interpretation forms no part of the nervous system,
> the system cannot be said to feel, learn, reason,
> et cetera. These are experiences or actions of the
> subject using his own neural processes.[58]

For the explication of the meaning of this experience, we
must return now to Polanyi's analysis of the ontological levels
of reality and apply this to the relationship of the mind to
the body. We may recall that every living entity is subject to
a dual control. Its lowest level is defined by the operational
principles articulated by physics and chemistry. The precise
way in which these principles can be applied is varied and cannot be determined by the principles themselves. This describes
the boundary conditions of physics and chemistry. Its highest
biotic level, then, controls these boundary conditions according to the operational principles of the living thing itself.
In every living entity, at least these two set of operational
principles function jointly, for the higher is not reducible to
the lower.

On the human level, mental operations, described by set
patterns which make up explicit thought and the integrative
powers of tacit knowing, function jointly with the principles
of human physiology to constitute an entity under dual control.
The mind then is a distinct ontological level in man which relies on the operational principles of the body while controlling the boundary conditions left indeterminate by these principles.[59]

This conception of man provides an explanation of the
meaning of human existence which avoids the dichotomies of a
radical dualism and a one-dimensional materialism by acknowledging the distinctive feature of man as a discrete ontological

level. The mind of man is not an extraneous entity added on to the body in some incomprehensible manner. The relationship between mind and body is simply one more instance of the dual control which functions between all successive ontological levels.[60] Furthermore, it demonstrates that we can come to know the reality of mind only by a personal judgment based on a tacit integration.[61] This follows from the general considerations of tacit knowing. In order to know the highest level of any entity, we must attempt to dwell in its particulars and tacitly integrate them into the focal whole which is described by the operational principles of its highest level. If we focus our attention solely on the operational principles of a lower level, we shall inevitably miss knowing the full significance of the reality.[62]

These considerations explain why a behaviorist description of man will never recognize the distinctiveness of the human mind. They show further that, though the operations of the mind normally will not disrupt the workings of the physiological (and physical and chemical) principles of the body, they can be radically affected by severe malfunctions of the body (such as brain damage). And finally they demonstrate that, "though rooted in the body, the mind is free in its actions--exactly as our common sense knows it to be free."[63]

The implications of the distinctive level of human consciousness for understanding the meaning of man may now be explored on the foundations provided by the logic of emergence. When the personal, linguistic, social, cultural, and historical elements of tacit knowing which were described in the preceding chapter are seen in light of this emergence, then knowledge itself, like every living activity, is a real achievement. The primary significance of this insight is that the human person and the knowledge he produces are ontologically grounded in a developmental process.

If we consider the ideal of total objectivity from this perspective, then it clearly must assume a knower outside the flow of history. This can be achieved only when time itself is atomized by conceiving it implicitly as a succession of "nows" through which the knower successively passes. In Polanyi's perspective, however, human knowledge can never be this detached, self-confirming truth encased in a static, a-temporal instant. Rather, it is a process directed from the real to an articulate expression of the real.

This can be clarified by recalling once more the structure of tacit knowing. Our knowledge is from the proximal to the distal term. This is to say, we know by reaching out of ourselves, our past achievements, toward the real, the focal point of our awareness, which is not yet but soon to be.[64] This means that the reality that man is at present can only be understood as the complex of interlocking achievements from his past, including his physical makeup, his social relationships, his cultural heritage, and his intellectual and moral standards directed toward their fulfillment.

Polanyi's conception of the ontological structure of reality as embedded in time and directed toward the future, including therefore the reality of human knowledge, has been expanded upon in light of some modern and contemporary expressions by Marjorie Grene. Since she is attempting to clarify this by referring to the analogies found in different perspectives, her expression is perhaps worth repeating.

> This principle is reminiscent of Heidegger. That, as one might say, the primary tense of existential time is future, is perhaps the central insight of *Sein und Zeit*; but the difference from my present thesis is significant. While Heidegger's future is the cessation of life, death only, Polanyi's unit of tacit knowing, or the parallel structure of comprehensive entities, comprises an open multiplicity of tensions—or, in Husserl's term, *protensions*, that is, ways in which the future pulls us toward it. In the yet unsolved problem, the developing embryo, the dance half-performed, the melody half-sung, the nesting behavior in course of enactment: everywhere in the living world the same future-drawn structure is evident. What spreads out before us here in the variety of life's achievements is not so much Heidegger's 'being to death' as Tillich's 'openness to the future.' Each protension, each foreshadowed end, is indeed definite and limited, and its achievement or the failure to achieve it will be definite and limited as well. Yet the number and variety of *kinds* of *telos* is open and unlimited. This principle is closer also to Whitehead; it is indeed equivalent to Whitehead's 'prehension,' or the lure of form as yet unrealized. It is the contrary equally of the Cartesian independent instant, and of the Newtonian absolute time which flows uniformly in one direction. Protensions

are temporal arches, curved times reaching back from
their goals to the steps that lead on to them.[65]

A further implication of this understanding of comprehensive entities whose reality is fashioned through a stretch of
time and from a matrix of overlapping relationships is that
values and meaning become ontologically grounded. When we
recognize any comprehensive entity, its reality is partially
determined by its surroundings, which, in turn, help to make
these surroundings what they are. A bird building its nest, to
use one of Grene's examples, is an activity which is susceptible of success or failure. Our attribution of success to a
particular instance of such an achievement is not simply a conventional imputation on our part. Granted Polanyi's understand-
ind of emergence and the distinctive reality of animal life,
then the action of the bird *is* successful within the context of
the physical, environmental, and biological determinants of the
bird's nest-building if it produces its intended results.

Such an appraisal of the ontological foundation of value
can be denied, of course, by reverting to an objectivist framework which attempts to conceive a one-dimensional world of isolated particulars randomly moving through discrete atomic moments of existence. But, as we have tried to argue in exposing
Polanyi's thought earlier in this work, this stance is logically
contradictory. Any sort of meaning given to a reality conceived as atomic can be upheld only by a prior tacit attribution of meaning to this very conception, even though such an
attribution is not explicitly allowed by the objectivist stance.
Once we recognize, on the other hand, that natural entities
constitute wholes which are not reducible to their constituent
parts and which are, accordingly, more real than their parts
because they manifest higher modes of existence, then we are
compelled to recognize also the reality of their achievements
and failures. Polanyi has specifically asserted this:

> The stratification of reality that is revealed here
> can be directly recognized by recalling that an act
> of comprehension invariably appreciates the coher-
> ence of that which it comprehends. This lends dis-
> tinctive *values* to things belonging to levels above
> that of natural inanimate objects. We judge ma-
> chines and the physiological operations of living
> beings to be either in working order or out of

order, and at the level of appetitive-perceptive
centres we exercise, in addition to this appraisal,
the assessment of rightness and error.[66]

The most significant consequence of Polanyi's reformulation of how man knows is thus the reinstatement of the hierarchical structure of reality which traditional ontology had always held. We can recognize real comprehensive entities, and
in this recognition we discover, as well as create, values.
This provides an intelligible and meaningful foundation for our
recognition of the multiplicity of forms of being with their
appropriate structure of dual control without the liabilities
of either an ontological dualism or a materialism (with its
implicit one-dimensional metaphysics).[67] This conception allows us, then, to recognize not only the distinctive center of
human individuality, but also a scheme whereby we can situate
it in the unfolding of emergence.

The mind of man, accordingly, develops through its own
hierarchical frameworks and relationships which are real, just
as in the case of the evolutionary antecedents sketched above.
In every act of knowledge, the person modifies his mental existence at least to some degree by incorporating the particulars of the reality in order to rely on them subsidiarily to
focus on their coherent feature.[68] Furthermore, since every
act of knowing is an indwelling, the frameworks described in
our tacit horizons include standards and criteria through which
our mental life is actualized. Any particular form of indwelling is thus a particular way of being a human person. This ontologically grounds human articulate systems and at the same
time recognizes that man's social relationships will determine
his conscious mode of existence.[69] It does not follow from
this, however, that man is totally determined by the frameworks
in which he exists. What does follow is that, if a judgment
compels us to accept a new framework, this is a corresponding
change in our way of being because the framework in which we
dwell has been altered.[70]

The basis for such existential choices we have already
indicated in the discussion of universal intent and shall try
to clarify it further through an analysis of truth in the next
section. At present it points to a significant feature in

Polanyi's understanding of man. Throughout the life-long process of tacit knowing a person develops himself in conjunction
with the opportunities provided by his cultural indwelling.
If he takes advantage to the fullest of the potential afforded
by this indwelling, he actualizes a self-striving toward an
ever greater comprehension of the real. In this self-actuali-
zation he is guided ultimately by principles of responsibility
which transcend even the intellectual operations of the mind.
The emergence of these principles and man's ability to be
guided by them are one of his distinguishing characteristics,
indicating a new stage in the evolutionary process which had
been previously dominated by simple self-perservation.[71] This
means that, just as the mind controls the boundary conditions
of the body, so too a person's mind itself unfolds through a
sequence of rising principles culminating in his responsible
judgments.[72]

When they are seen in light of emergence, our standards
for responsible judgment are also provided with ontological
significance. Insofar as all men strive toward the comprehension of the real, this activity includes not only their subjective tastes and physical environment, but also the social
community which establishes a hierarchy of both individual and
cultural structures. Man's responsible judgments must take
this socially structured reality into account if they are to
be a valid expression of what is in fact the case. As a result, "not only goals, but *meanings*, which are prior to goals,
acquire an ontological reality in reference to which life is
not only, by us, interpreted, but *is*."[73]

At the conclusion of the last chapter we introduced Polanyi's notion of a heuristic field which activated a gradient
for discovery, and claimed that this described a "society of
explorers" searching for the potential meaning embodied in our
cultural traditions. The exposition of the logic of emergence
may be understood, finally, to provide an ontological basis
for this conception also. Polanyi has attempted to clarify
this relationship between emergence and human thought by comparing some forces which control inanimate nature with the processes of growth in human knowledge. Generally speaking, the
developments produced by inanimate nature may be understood to

include these three characteristics: "(1) We see forces driving toward stabler potentialities; (2) catalysts or accidental releasers of friction-locked forces cause them to actualize these potentialities; and (3) such accidents may be uncaused events subject only to probable tendencies."[74] The achievements of man resemble these characteristics in that a problem may be evoked by potentialities in the cultural framework leading to a more stable configuration represented by the choice of a solution. And, as in the case of radioactive decomposition, this choice is comparable to uncaused mechanical events, guided only by a framework which leaves the direction of the solution indeterminate. Nevertheless, the intervention of the activity of the knower specifies at the same time how discoveries differ from the inanimate developments: "(1) the field evoking and guiding them is not that of a more stable configuration but of a problem; (2) their occurrence is not spontaneous but due to an effort toward the actualization of certain hidden potentialities; and (3) the uncaused action which evokes them is usually an imaginative thrust toward discovering these potentialities."[75]

In this way Polanyi has attempted to integrate the human powers of thought into the framework of an evolutionary emergence. Through his reformulation of the outlines for an ontology of evolution, knowing mind once again becomes a natural entity without being absorbed back into that from which it emerged. In light of his efforts, the meaning of man may be described as man's radical openness in the process of history toward an ever more comprehensive discovery of reality.

D. *The Discovery of Reality*

The aim of this chapter so far has been to uncover the ontological structures implied in the theory of personal knowledge--with respect to both the knower and the known. This analysis was required so that neither the subject of knowledge nor the scope of the object toward which the subject's attention might be directed would be needlessly truncated by a priori assumptions. The previous sections of this chapter could then be considered as an extended, though necessary, excursus. Its purpose was two-fold: to clarify the meaning of

Polanyi's understanding of reality so that any objections to it could be viewed from this more comprehensive perspective; and then, once this vantage point had been grasped, to enable us to demonstrate that human knowledge, though always perspectival and embedded in historical process, is nevertheless of reality and can accordingly make a claim to truth.

Since the force of our argument required that Polanyi's understanding of reality be outlined first of all in its general features, some important precisions were temporarily bypassed for the sake of achieving this comprehensive view. Now that this has been accomplished, a more detailed analysis is possible and reveals that there are several distinct nuances to this understanding of our knowledge of reality which depend on the point of emphasis in a particular context. Our goal of validating Polanyi's contention, that our knowledge is a comprehension of that which is real, will be aided by delineating four of these interdependent senses in which he uses the term reality.[76]

The primordial sense of reality, upon which Polanyi grounds the other senses of the term in the exposition of his thought, is that which exists independently of our focal or explicit knowledge of it. In this first sense, reality serves as the external pole of all our personal affirmations made with universal intent.[77] This means that all our claims to truth which are expressed through our articulate judgments must be grounded on the real. Implied in this notion, however, is the recognition that truth admits to degrees of realization in expression dependent on the context within which our affirmations àre made. This is so both with regard to historical development and to frameworks which presumably penetrate the reality more profoundly. Thus within the scientific horizon, relativity physics expresses the quantifiable properties of nature more comprehensively than Newtonian physics and is in this sense "more true." Both make their truth claims in reference to reality viewed from the same fundamental framework which has developed in the course of history. Similarly today one could say that empirical psychology provides a more adequate understanding of man than chemistry because its concern is such that it penetrates the reality of man more profoundly than a

simple chemical analysis. This means that, even though they
both operate from within an empirical perspective, a psychological description of the neurophysiology of man presumably goes
beyond his chemical properties because it penetrates a higher
level in man.

Unfortunately, when reality has this primordial sense in
Polanyi's thought, it functions more as a description of the
claim that we know the real rather than an explanation of how
we do know it. This sense of reality, in other words, does
not provide any immediate criteria for our judging that a particular affirmation made with universal intent does in fact relate to reality as its objective pole.

A second sense for Polanyi's understanding of reality may
be uncovered in the phrase, "aspect of reality."[78] When this
phrase appears in Polanyi's writings, it generally is used in
conjunction with the first sense. On the other hand it bears
a resemblance to the next two senses we shall examine. Consequently the precise meaning with which Polanyi intends to endow this phrase is not completely clear. Nevertheless since he
uses it primarily in the context of scientific knowledge, he
probably is intending to establish the ontological validity of
science by acknowledging that the quantifiable properties of
reality (in the first sense) are aspects of reality. Thus the
scientific framework illuminates the meaning of reality by explaining an aspect of reality. This obviously counters the
various forms of positivism, idealism, and instrumentalism by
claiming that a scientist knows an aspect of reality. It likewise points to the inadequacy of the application of the scientific understanding to an aspect of reality for which it is
not suited. The problem with this second sense of reality,
however, is that it does not, of itself, provide a sufficient
explanation of our ability to know an aspect of reality through
science nor of Polanyi's recognition that science is not applicable to some other aspects of reality.

A third sense of reality found in Polanyi's thought is
much more significant for our purposes: this is the recognition of the levels of reality or, expressed in classical terms,
degrees of being. If Polanyi's arguments against all forms of
implicit metaphysical reductivism, which were outlined in the

previous section, have any validity whatsoever, then he is
clearly affirming that there are levels in reality which we
know. The importance of this third sense of reality obviously
consists in the fact that we have here an understanding of reality which requires us to move beyond the merely phenomenal
to a knowledge of reality which is, in the traditional sense,
metaphysical. There remains, however, the task of providing
an explanation of how we do know such levels of reality represented by life and human thought. This shall be our concern
shortly.

The fourth sense of reality found in Polanyi's thought is
his comparative use of the term. As we have already seen,[79]
in this sense it functions as a criterion, where the ability
of something to manifest itself in new and unexpected ways is
a sign of its degree of reality. In light of this delineation
of the first three senses for reality in Polanyi's thought,
the meaning of this comparative use of reality is more firmly
established. Through it the interconnectedness of the first
three senses is also clarified. Whenever one thing is asserted
to be more real than something else, it clearly implies that
this is grounded objectively as the external pole of our assertion and so is real (in sense one). Thus when an entity is
said to be more real in comparison with another entity, it implies both that it is a higher level of reality (sense three)
and that it is real independently of our knowing it (sense one).
Also a scientific theory may be said to be more real than an
instance of what it is describing because it heightens our perception by disclosing an aspect of reality (sense two) in the
particular reality (sense one) which, in turn, will lead to
future and novel manifestations of aspects of reality presently unknown or even unthinkable.

Lest this be misunderstood, a useful distinction, offered
by Marjorie Grene in her defense of Polanyi's criterion of reality, may be introduced at this point.[80] An objection to
Polanyi's criterion of reality might be raised by maintaining
that it is confusing the artificial with the natural, or that
it is making the conventional more real than the factual. If
the criterion were applied to two different natural entities
which comprise two distinct levels of reality (sense three),

there would be no great difficulty concerning its intent,
though some would doubt that it ever could be applied. But
when it is a question of human constructs, the matter is not so
clear. What can it mean to claim, for example, that a painting
is more real than that which it depicts, or a scientific theory
more real than nature? Such an objection can be clarified,
suggests Grene, by distinguishing different dimensions in reality. Polanyi's criterion is calling our attention to the
"depth" or "intensity" of being. This is distinguishable from
"facticity," the fact of existence or non-existence, which is
a linear, "extensive" dimension of being. In this sense, then,
a painting could express a dimension of the depth of reality
which goes beyond any extensive dimension of which we are normally aware.[81] The problem with Polanyi's criterion arises,
in other words, because the implicit understanding of reality
which predominates in the objectivist framework is the linear,
extensive dimension as the only proper sense of reality. For
Polanyi, on the other hand, reality cannot be so constricted
because it is much richer and includes the realm of "fact" as
one aspect of the reality we know alongside many other dimensions which reveal the depth of reality, including all living
things and their achievements.

While these clarifications may be quite helpful for understanding Polanyi's thought, it still remains to be explained
how we do know reality in any of the senses just delineated.
Unfortunately, there is no thoroughly explicit treatment of
this problem in Polanyi's writings. Indeed, the fourth sense
of reality, which accredits something as possessing a deeper
reality because it can manifest itself indefinitely in the
future, could be interpreted as an attempt to evade the problem. According to such an interpretation, Polanyi's criterion
of reality would be understood to be formulating a test of
fruitfulness in a positivist or pragmatic sense. To do so,
however, would be not only a failure to situate this in the
context of Polanyi's thought as a whole, but also a miscon-
ception of the criterion itself. The fruitfulness of a theory
seems to work as a way of conceiving its truth only because
the theory does in some sense correspond to reality. A theory
is proposed not because it is now fruitful (which can only be

demonstrated in the future), but because it is held to be true and implicitly, then, a correct understanding of reality. If the theory is true, it will be fruitful precisely because it discloses an aspect of reality existing independently of us and capable of revealing itself to us in novel ways in the future.[82]

The significance of these few remarks begins to bear greater importance when they are placed in the larger context of the problem of our knowledge of the real. Since for Polanyi knowledge which is true is based upon a grasp of the real, an analysis of his understanding of truth should provide a clue to any validation of our knowledge of reality which is implied in his thought. Accordingly, we must briefly attempt to present Polanyi's understanding of truth as the final consideration necessary to expose any implied explanation which could substantiate his claim that we know reality.

The discussion above clearly indicates that Polanyi understands truth to be the expression of a relation between a personal affirmation made with universal intent and some objective reality. It is equally clear, moreover, that the process whereby this occurs cannot be understood according to the "correspondence theory of truth" as it is espoused in much of contemporary philosophy. Early in this study we noted how the objectivist framework, because it does not admit the judgment of the person to enter into the act of knowledge, results in an "objectivist dilemma" where truth, at least as Bertrand Russell expressed it, consists in the coincidence between subjective beliefs and an actual fact.[83] Polanyi points out that the possibility for these two terms ever coinciding cannot be explained consistently from within the objectivist framework. If the personal affirmation is discounted in the knowing situation as providing the basis for establishing such a relationship, then there is no way in which we can even speak of any supposed "facts" without an infinite regress.

If we wish to avoid such a regress and arrive at an adequate understanding of truth, we are required, in Polanyi's estimation, to acknowledge the necessary participation of the knower. What this means can be seen from a consideration of an ordinary factual claim. When we say that a factual statement is true, Polanyi explains that what we are doing is making an articulate assertion which "is composed of two parts: a sentence conveying the content of what is asserted and a tacit act by which this sentence is asserted."[84] The articulate assertion itself may thus be separated from the act of assertion in order to test it by some criteria. If it stands up to the required evidence, the original assertion may then be repeated and judged again to be true. But the act of judging itself is not composed of two parts. Since it is an act which the knower is performing, it establishes a relationship between the knower and that which is known through the articulate expression. The act of knowing a reality and expressing it adequately is something the person is doing, not observing.[85]

According to Polanyi's analysis, then, truth can only be known by an intelligent affirmation expressing the relationship of the knower to the reality of that which is known. Only because the predominant contemporary explanation of the correspondence theory of truth leaves out the subject and the reality or being of the thing known does it gain a semblance of credibility.[86] We have already seen that to do so is logically contradictory. Because of this objectivist understanding of the correspondence theory of truth, Polanyi calls his understanding a "redefinition" of truth.[87] We would submit, however, that Polanyi's analysis is in fact a redefinition only in the context of contemporary thought and recovers the classical metaphysical understanding of the adequacy of thought and the being of a particular thing.[88]

If the personal affirmation is that which relates the knower with the reality of the thing known, then our contention, that Polanyi's understanding of knowledge provides an explanation of how we know the real, can be substantiated only by an analysis of the process whereby a person in fact makes a judgment which he asserts to be true. Or expressed negatively, the claim that we know the real can never be demonstrated impersonally.

This same conclusion is just as forcefully advanced if we consider what is meant by our knowledge of the real. We have already seen the nuances which the term reality possesses in Polanyi's thought. It follows that, unless we wish to be

dogmatic and erect a notion of metaphysical knowledge which
would be a priori impossible to achieve, we must recognize similar nuances when we attempt to understand what the claim that
we know reality means. In the course of his analysis of Polanyi's contribution to the understanding of metaphysical knowledge, Edward Pols has performed this task admirably. In order to situate his observations, we may point out that if our
knowledge is to be of "reality" or "an aspect of reality," or
if it opens us to "levels of reality" or to entities which are
"more real," then it must in some sense go beyond Kantian
phenomena. The question, accordingly, is this: in what sense
does the "appearance" of something lead to a knowledge of reality in that appearance? In this context Pols makes the following comments:

> Kant, in erecting the thing-in-itself as an impos-
> sible ideal toward which we might turn if we were
> provided with an intellectual intuition, almost
> persuades us that this is what metaphysicians have
> always been after. Yet few, if any, philosophers
> have ever claimed that it was within our capacity
> to know an absolute reality unqualified by a rela-
> tion to realities of lesser degree. No doubt if
> someone should want to possess a transcendence so
> pure as to be isolated from all the manifestations
> that depend upon it, Kant gives him good reasons
> why he cannot have it. But we have a right to hope
> for a knowledge that should yield us *something* of
> the domain that he held inaccessible to reason.
> Certainly we shall not settle for less and still
> wish to call it metaphysical knowledge. It should
> yield us something of the absolute *in* the relative;
> transcendence *in and through* the particulars it
> transcends; the really real *refracted* in various
> degrees of reality; Being *appearing* to us in ap-
> pearances. If we look for pure Reality in the
> sense of a thing-in-itself we shall certainly find
> pure Nothing: nothing happening; nothing at issue;
> no diversity, but instead a stolid and inane Unity.
> It clears our minds to be persuaded of the impos-
> sibility of this extreme case, even if there are
> some of us who can honestly say that we have never
> been tempted to look in that direction. And we are
> convincingly taught by Kant that, if there are more
> profitable directions to look in, there is profit
> there only if our glance is simultaneously upon the
> nature of our own cognitive powers.[89]

Just as in the case of our true judgments, so also here in our
knowledge of reality we are driven back to the bedrock of the
experience of ourselves as knowers for the source of any

validation.

The requirements of our inquiry lead us to examine again the human mode of knowing, but now for the purposes of exposing any conditions which enable us to know the real and judge truly. This clearly does not imply any attempt to establish an explicit knowledge of "reality-in-itself" or judgments which embody "eternal truths." The modern understanding of intelligibility demonstrates the explicit content of all human affirmations is not the absolute and necessary. Rather, there is an experience of the dimension of ultimacy[90] which qualifies all our intelligent activity and which functions as the condition enabling us to know in any sense whatsoever. In relation to this experience of ultimacy we do know the real in the contingent, the truth in the manifold of relativity. Polanyi's analysis of the human mode of knowing uncovers at least three moments where such a dimension of ultimacy can be experienced in our conscious life. In the concretely existing knowing subject, they operate concurrently are are thus susceptible to analysis only at the risk of distortion. Nevertheless, if this warning is kept in mind, we can discover the dimension of ultimacy on the basis of which our historically conditioned and relative judgments are made in these experiences: (1) the tacit foreknowledge of reality grounding every judgment, (2) the rational power of regulative principles derived from our cultural frameworks, and (3) the intellectual passions leading us to an ever more adequate comprehension and discovery of reality.

Through his analysis of the structure of tacit knowing, Polanyi recognized in the ontological aspect of every act of knowledge a condition for the possibility of all human knowledge of reality. While this tacit reference to the real is always present, it normally goes unnoticed because we are relying on it to focus on a particular entity or some aspect of reality. The moment when this element of our cognitional activity most profoundly impinges upon our conscious experience is in the paradigm case of knowledge, in our knowledge of a good problem leading eventually to a new discovery.

The context in which Polanyi first uncovered this dimension of ultimacy was, of course, his appraisal of scientific discovery. Very early in his study of the scientific enterprise

Polanyi pointed out that "the scientist's intuition can integrate widely dispersed data, camouflaged by sundry irrelevant
connexions, and indeed seek out such data by experiments guided
by a dim foreknowledge of the possibilities which lie ahead."[91]
Years later, after having grappled with the implications of
this insight for actual scientific discoveries, Polanyi was
able to clarify this process even further by providing an analogy from physics:

> I have spoken of our powers to perceive a coher-
> ence bearing on reality, with its yet hidden future
> manifestations. But there exists also a more intense-
> ly pointed knowledge of hidden coherence: the kind
> of foreknowledge we call a problem. And we know that
> the scientist produces problems, has hunches, and,
> elated by these anticipations, pursues the quest that
> should fulfill these anticipations. This quest is
> guided throughout by feelings of a deepening coher-
> ence and these feelings have a fair chance of proving
> right. We may recognize here the powers of a dynamic
> intuition.
> The mechanism of this power can be illuminated
> by an analogy. Physics speaks of potential energy
> that is released when a weight slides down a slope.
> Our search for deeper coherence is likewise guided
> by a potentiality. We feel the slope toward deeper
> insight as we feel the direction in which a heavy
> weight is pulled along a steep incline. It is this
> dynamic intuition which guides the pursuit of dis-
> covery.[92]

There are two significant features contained in this analysis of the process of scientific discovery. The first is that
the experience of ultimacy, in the form of a potentially deeper
coherence, is guiding the scientist toward his comprehension
of the as yet unknown reality. Secondly, moreover, it implies
that this tacit foreknowledge is operative precisely because
it is cognitive. As we saw earlier in this study, this cognitive foreknowledge is required by the logic of our knowledge
of problems. In order for a scientist to pursue a discovery,
he must have an awareness of what he is looking for, which is
at the same time not yet explicit or focal. Such a paradox,
which constitutes our knowledge of a problem, "makes sense if
we admit that we can have a tacit foreknowledge of yet undis-
covered things."[93] By means of this tacit foreknowledge of
the reality he is seeking, the creative scientist experiences
a dimension of ultimacy in his conscious research which guides

him toward an explicit formulation.

While the primary locus for Polanyi's analysis of this foreknowledge of the real in our intellectual activity is science, its operation is applicable universally in all human knowledge.[94] That Polanyi understands this to be operative in all our acts of knowledge is clear from his explicit assertions and from the requirements of the consistency of his thought as a whole. For example, in the context of our ability to comprehend novel elements of our experience by understanding their joint meaning, he declares that "our active foreknowledge of an unknown entity is the right motive and guide of knowing in all our mental endeavors."[95] In another case, which we have already discussed in a different context, Polanyi explains that our use of general conceptions requires a foreknowledge which allows us to integrate tacitly new instances to which the term can refer. In this explanation he remarks that, while it is more evident in some cases, such foreknowledge is "never quite absent from the act of knowing."[96] Finally in the context of his criterion of reality, Polanyi maintains that our recognition of the depth of an entity is derived from the experience of ultimacy based on our tacit foreknowledge that the reality does have this depth and thus can reveal itself in novel ways in the future; and "this is to class our knowledge of reality with the kind of foreknowledge which guides scientists to discovery."[97]

In addition to these explicit assertions found in Polanyi's writings, a consideration of the structure of tacit knowing in the framework of emergence shows that, if knowledge is always an activity, something we do, then this "from-to" or vectorial quality of tacit knowing presupposes such a tacit foreknowledge of the real. What tacit knowing is "from" is described by the ontological aspect of its structure, and its directedness "towards" is experienced both as a foreknowledge of the real and an explicit comprehension of an aspect or degree of reality grounded in this foreknowledge.[98]

Flowing from this, the second dimension of ultimacy in our cognitive experience is to be found in the cultural heritage by means of which we develop our mental existence. Our cultural heritage is composed of articulate frameworks or intellectual horizons which provide the conditions for our application of explicit methods, norms, axioms, and the like. They form the general ontological conceptions implicit in any given intellectual inquiry. We know the world in an explicit way by thinking *through* them, not *about* them. As such they are not, indeed cannot be, the subject of explicit, formal demonstration.

Polanyi analyzes this dimension of ultimacy in terms of the structure of commitment where the personal and the universal meet in responsible judgment. "Here the personal comes into existence by asserting universal intent, and the universal is constituted by being accepted as the impersonal term of this personal commitment."[99] As a result of these interacting forces of our intellectual life, the personal act of knowing includes as a condition for its concrete actualization the element of compulsion or determination which is experienced in the form of the responsibility permeating our judgments about reality.[100] By committing ourselves to the intellectual horizons of our cultural heritage and acting in the world in light of them, we come into being as persons through a conscious separation of ourselves from the contingent flow of immediate events in the world. This can be achieved because the premisses implied in such a commitment function as a demand on our responsibility and thus are normative.[101]

Through our reliance on these articulate frameworks we then make our explicit claims to truth. Because of our commitments to the universal standards of our articulate frameworks, Polanyi likens such judgments to Kant's analysis of morality.[102] But there is a major difference in that committing ourselves to these "regulative principles" derived from our intellectual frameworks, we now are affirming them to be true and thus to be an adequate means of understanding certain aspects of the reality under consideration.[103] In order to acknowledge the validity of this explanation, it is necessary to keep in mind that the tacit reference to reality is operating simultaneously with our explicit affirmations.[104] The human mode of knowing is thus empowered to break the flow of relativity in affirming the truth of a particular aspect of reality in light of an intellectual horizon to which it is committed.

It does so even though the truth affirmed is contingent and provisional, not absolute or necessary. This dimension of ultimacy is present in our affirmations about reality in the sense that, given a historical framework and the personal responsibility seeking universal intent, all the demands of rationality have been at this moment fulfilled. This enables us to affirm, "Such is *in fact* the case," with respect to a particular situation, *not* that it is *necessarily* the case. We can then give our reasons for affirming why we say something is true, though these reasons can never be fully specifiable.[105]

The third dimension of ultimacy is experienced in what Polanyi terms our "intellectual passions."[106] They energize our mental life by filling us with a drive to understand which is objective and universal in intent. These intellectual passions have a cognitive element insofar as they perform a selective function by upholding certain interests and values and discounting others. Closely associated with this is their heuristic function which accepts these values in order to probe more deeply into the meaning of reality from that perspective and which--in cases of marked originality--leads to the dwelling in a new framework with an altered set of values. And finally, these intellectual passions often will function persuasively in an attempt to convince others of the validity of a new or different framework.[107]

This drive to understand is experienced with its most profound force when we are struggling with a problem which finally becomes open to our comprehension. What happens in such instances is not the surcease of intellectual passion. Rather what occurs is the grasp of a new insight which is contemplated both in itself and in the expectations it raises that it will in its turn be filled with new implications for further development.[108]

Having examined these three dimensions of ultimacy from the vantage point of their distinctive moments in human consciousness, we can now turn to an appreciation of their significance in a more profound fashion by analyzing their joint operation, for it is in this way that they are experienced by the knowing subject. At this point we may say that our intellectual passions, which are grounded on the experience of

our tacit foreknowledge of the real and are fostered by our
historically conditioned intellectual horizons, lead us toward
an ever more explicit discovery of reality. Because of this
experience we can accept our cultural horizons with all their
limitations and weaknesses and still adhere to a quest for the
truth. The limited way in which we activate this quest will
define our particular form of personal existence and constitutes our "calling."[109] We can do this in full responsibility
by recognizing that, in spite of the fact that our culture is
embodied in limited horizons, it still opens us to various aspects of reality. Thus even though our explicit affirmations
never fully exhaust the reality of the thing in question, we
experience, in addition to the truth of the affirmation, a
tacit knowledge which is indeterminate and which goes beyond
the explicit content of the affirmation because it cannot yet
be explicitly stated.[110] In other words, we experience the
affirmation as grasping the real through a particular, historically conditioned horizon, knowing at the same time that the
aspect of reality we have explicitly grasped does not exhaust
its full significance.[111] Because of this we realize, finally,
that we can comprehend the reality of anything only in stages,
gradually opening its meaning to our explicit understanding.[112]

This leads to the conclusion that any truth we discover,
which is recognized only insofar as it has a bearing on reality, will be provisional and perspectival, but nevertheless
adequate in the context. By pursuing the real with the responsibility borne of universal intent, we grow as persons and
at the same time expand our cultural horizons into increasingly
adequate tools for the explicit comprehension of the real.
This process has been aptly described by Polanyi as follows:

> The intellectual daring which impels our acts of
> commitment retains its dynamic character within
> the state of commitment, in relying on its own
> resourcefulness to deal with the unspecifiable im-
> plications of the knowledge acquired by the act of
> commitment. In this self-reliance lies our ulti-
> mate power for keeping our heads in the face of
> a changing world. It makes us feel at home in a
> universe presenting us with a succession of un-
> precedented situations and even makes us enjoy
> life best precisely on these occasions, which
> force us to respond to novelty by reinterpreting
> our accepted knowledge.[113]

The question which now can be raised from the inquiries
initiated in this chapter concerns the significance of this dimension of ultimacy making human knowledge possible and the ultimate meaning of emergence. On the one hand, this dimension
of ultimacy does not result from any effort of our knowing;
rather it is experienced as the condition transcending all our
explicit affirmations. This dimension of ultimacy, which is
encountered at the core of our self-awareness, provides the
foundation that allows us to trust in our ability to know the
truth provisionally and to hope that we shall discover it fully.
On the other hand, the ultimate reference toward which our knowing strives is reality, but only insofar as it is known by way
of a tacit foreknowledge. It is this transcendent reality which
provides the ground in light of which we are able to comprehend
the meaning of the contingent reality of our focal awareness and
to believe that the meaning will be fulfilled in a way that is
still incomprehensible.

In each pole of this experience our foundational inquiry
throws us open to mystery--that which grounds our proximate
norms of intelligibility and which draws us ever deeper into
itself. Our inquiry has thus led to the conclusion that this
openness to mystery, which is the source of an inexhaustible
intelligibility,[114] constitutes the ultimate meaning of man and
the final goal of emergence. This appears to be the inescap-
able exigency of our inquiry. As it stands, however, this conclusion is ambiguous. Nevertheless, we would submit, echoing
the sentiments of Polanyi, that the recognition of the validity
of this hope[115] and this belief[116] establishes a basis for religious faith. For if the depths of mystery, in light of which
we know and toward which we are drawn, can be approached in any
sense, it will only be through religious discourse.

NOTES TO CHAPTER IV

1. *Personal Knowledge*, "Preface" to the Torchbook Edition, p. xi and *The Tacit Dimension*, p. x.

2. See also Marjorie Grene, "Tacit Knowing and the Pre-Reflective Cogito," p. 40 and "Introduction" to *Knowing and Being*, p. xiv for a similar appraisal. For the antecedent understanding of human knowledge which anticipated this later development, see above pp. 28-31.

3. Polanyi has described this functional operation of tacit knowing and the aspects which flow from it in several of his later works: *The Tacit Dimension*, pp. 9-13; "On Body and Mind," 198-199; "Science and Man's Place in the Universe," pp. 57-61; "The Logic of Tacit Inference," p. 141; and "The Structure of Consciousness," p. 212.

4. See Marjorie Grene, "Tacit Knowing and the Pre-Reflective Cogito," p. 38.

5. See "The Logic of Tacit Inference," pp. 138-158.

6. "The Structure of Consciousness," p. 213.

7. *The Tacit Dimension*, pp. 95-96, n. 1; "The Creative Imagination," 86; "Sense-Giving and Sense-Reading," p. 194; and "The Structure of Consciousness," p. 212.

8. See note 3 above.

9. See Thomas Kuhn, *The Structure of Scientific Revolutions*, pp. 62-72, 85-86, and 98-99. For other examples, see *Personal Knowledge*, pp. 152-158.

10. "Tacit Knowing: Its Bearing on Some Problems of Philosophy," pp. 173f.

11. See note 3 above.

12. Insofar as this is an interpretation of classical epistemology, the question obviously is far from being settled. Perhaps it is sufficient to note that this interpretation of traditional metaphysics is characteristic of the "transcendental" or "dynamic" school of Thomism. See, for example, Victor Preller, *Divine Science and the Science of God*, pp. 54-55, where he has this to say on the semantic aspect of knowledge: "We may say that the formal significance of the language we use to describe reality derives from the rules and principles of the conceptual system we find ourselves using to interpret experience, while the referential or semantical content of that language (the 'matter' of the language) derives from the experience on the basis of which we use the language to refer to reality. That is the explanation, I believe, of Aquinas' claim that the world

as (non-intentionally) experienced is only potentially intelligible and must be made actually intelligible by the
judgments of the intellect. To say that 'being' is 'intelligible' is to say that ultimately 'that which is' can
be measured in terms created by intellect, not that intellect is measured by norms discoverable in 'that which
is.'"

13. *The Tacit Dimension*, pp. x-xi; see also "The Logic of
Tacit Inference," p. 141.

14. See note 3 above.

15. William H. Poteat, "Myths, Stories, History, Eschatology
and Action: Some Polanyian Meditations," in *Intellect
and Hope*, p. 203.

16. *Ibid.*, p. 204. Poteat adds to this reflection the following instructive note (n. 6): "This elucidation must
strike non-philosophers as at best an ingenious feat devised to triumph over a difficulty which common sense
would never allow to arise. This is in fact the case.
But philosophy in the modern period and the sciences and
even theory-laden common sense which get their own theories about knowing and doing *from* this philosophic tradition are so ubiquitously infected by this 'subjunctiv-
itis' that only a more radical form of reflection can
overcome it!"

17. "The Logic of Tacit Inference," p. 141.

18. For typical statements of this process by Polanyi, see
the following: *Science, Faith and Society*, p. 23; *The
Tacit Dimension*, pp. 24, 68; "From Copernicus to Ein-
stein," 56; "Problem Solving," 98 and 101; "Faith and
Reason," 244; "The Creative Imagination," 86-88; and in
Knowing and Being, "The Republic of Science," p. 55 and
"The Growth of Science in Society," pp. 79-80.

19. *The Tacit Dimension*, pp. 30-31.

20. *Ibid.*, pp. 32-33.

21. See the introduction to the 1964 edition of *Science, Faith
and Society*, p. 10 and in *Knowing and Being* the following
articles: "The Unaccountable Element in Science," pp.
119-120; "The Logic of Tacit Inference," p. 141; and
"Tacit Knowing: Its Bearing on Some Problems of Philosophy," pp. 168, 172. It should be pointed out here that
this comparative understanding of the real is an explicit
formulation of what was implied in Polanyi's earlier writings. For some of these earlier expressions, see *Personal
Knowledge*, pp. 5, 43, 103-104, 117, 130, 147, 189, 327-
331, and 392; "From Copernicus to Einstein," 56; "Problem
Solving," 101; "The Creative Imagination," 93; and "Faith
and Reason," 244.

22. *The Tacit Dimension*, pp. 33-34. The original is italicized.

23. See *The Study of Man*, pp. 47-51; *Personal Knowledge*, pp. 328-331; "Life Transcending Physics and Chemistry," 57-59; *The Tacit Dimension*, pp. 38-40; and in *Knowing and Being*, "The Logic of Tacit Inference," pp. 153-154; "Tacit Knowing: Its Bearing on Some Problems of Philosophy," pp. 175-176; "The Structure of Consciousness," pp. 216-218; and "Life's Irreducible Structure," pp. 225, 231-232.

24. "Life's Irreducible Structure," p. 227.

25. *Ibid.*, p. 228.

26. *The Tacit Dimension*, p. 40.

27. "The Structure of Consciousness," p. 217.

28. *The Tacit Dimension*, pp. 39-40 and "The Structure of Consciousness," pp. 217-218.

29. "Tacit Knowing: Its Bearing on Some Problems of Philosophy," pp. 175-176. Polanyi underscores in this article (p. 180, no. 10) how the purpose of a machine is often decisive for its identification with this case. "Some years ago Phillips (Eindhoven) and United Incandescent Lamp (Ujpest) were in conflict about the question whether the newly invented sodium discharge lamps were to be classed as 'neon lights' under an agreement to which both firms were parties. An important point made for *not* classing them thus was that sodium lights are used for *seeing by them* and neon lights for *being seen*." The salient feature of this illustration is that the purpose of the discovery, not primarily its physical components, was able to resolve a contractual dispute. This implies, in Polanyi's terms, that there is a distinct level which defines a machine and which is irreducible to the lower level which it controls.

30. "Science and Man's Place in the Universe," p. 70.

31. See *The Tacit Dimension*, pp. 41-42 and "Life Transcending Physics and Chemistry," 55.

32. "Life Transcending Physics and Chemistry," 61.

33. Polanyi's more rigorous and detailed statement of this innovative argument may be found in his articles, "Life Transcending Physics and Chemistry," 62-64 and "Life's Irreducible Structure," pp. 227-230, and in his remarks delivered in the symposium published under the title, "Do Life Processes Transcend Physics and Chemistry?" *Zygon*, III (1968), 444-447.

34. "Life Transcending Physics and Chemistry," 64.

35. "Life's Irreducible Structure," p. 235.

36. "Polanyi makes this point because this type of an understanding of irreducibility is incorrectly assumed by some

biologists, such as Barry Commoner, to be sufficient to account for the distinctive reality of life. See "Life Transcending Physics and Chemistry," 56-57.

37. "Life's Irreducible Structure," p. 231.

38. *The Tacit Dimension*, p. 45.

39. *Ibid.*, pp. 46-48. A thorough explanation of this process would also include a systematic way of understanding a creative agency to account for these innovations, such as the theories of Bergson, Teilhard, and Whitehead propose. Since our concern is primarily methodological, this kind of explanation will not be attempted here. For our purpose the minimal requirements for recognizing the distinctive features of life, including eventually man, will provide a sufficient basis for dealing with the foundational problem of man's religious beliefs.

40. In *The Tacit Dimension* (p. 48) Polanyi suggests the use of the term ideogenesis to refer to the more restricted causal sequence of the individual growth in order to distinguish it from the normally analyzed statistical sequence of phylogenesis.

41. For the detailed exposition of Polanyi's argument leading to this conclusion, see Chapter 13 of *Personal Knowledge*, especially pp. 393-402.

42. "Knowing and Being," p. 135.

43. "The Logic of Tacit Inference," p. 152.

44. *Ibid.*, p. 151.

45. See *Personal Knowledge*, pp. 363-364, 378 and *The Tacit Dimension*, p. 51.

46. *The Tacit Dimension*, pp. 48-49, 55.

47. "The Logic of Tacit Inference," p. 152. See also "Logic and Psychology," 34 and *The Tacit Dimension*, pp. 29-32.

48. See *The Study of Man*, pp. 65-66, 71.

49. See "On Body and Mind," 202-203 and "Logic and Psychology," 34-35.

50. For Polanyi's discussion of Ryle's argument, see "Logic and Psychology," 34 and "The Structure of Consciousness," pp. 222-223. In the latter article Polanyi makes an interesting comparison between Ryle's position and the phenomenological stance of Merleau-Ponty. Polanyi contends that there is a remarkable agreement in both positions insofar as they reject any dualistic analysis of the human person. But then the problem reasserts itself: Ryle's assumptions do not allow him to recognize the reality of mind, whereas Merleau-Ponty does by an appeal

to "existential experience." This dilemma can be resolved only by a more fundamental clarification, such as that offered by the theory of tacit knowledge and the ontological levels of existence, so that the insights of both can be appreciated.

51. See Marjorie Grene, *The Knower and the Known*, pp. 241-242.

52. See "The Structure of Consciousness," p. 214; "Life's Irreducible Structure," p. 238; and "Logic and Psychology," 29.

53. The particular points in the discussion which follows are examined in "Logic and Psychology," 38.

54. *Ibid.*, p. 39.

55. "The Structure of Consciousness," p. 219.

56. "The Logic of Tacit Inference," p. 147.

57. "Logic and Psychology," 39.

58. "On Body and Mind," 202.

59. "The Structure of Consciousness," pp. 218-222 and "Logic and Psychology," 39-40.

60. "The Logic of Tacit Inference," p. 155.

61. *Ibid.*, p. 151.

62. "The Structure of Consciousness," p. 221.

63. "Logic and Psychology," 40.

64. See Grene, *The Knower and the Known*, p. 244 and her "Introduction" to *Knowing and Being*, p. xi. See also Karl Rahner's remarks in *Spirit in the World*, p. 111: "Therefore, the motion takes hold of each of its moments only insofar as it is from and toward its end. The present of the motion (its momentary state) is thus a vindication of its past in reaching-out-towards the future, and only in this reaching-out-of-the-past-into-the-future does the present maintain itself." This understanding of a "now" as actual only insofar as it strives toward and derives from an end provides a striking convergence with Polanyi's understanding of the ontological character of time from a different tradition.

65. *The Knower and the Known*, p. 245.

66. *The Study of Man*, pp. 58-59. See also Marjorie Grene's amplifications of this aspect of Polanyi's thought in *The Knower and the Known*, pp. 202-217 (which she has substantially adapted from her earlier article, "The Logic of Biology," in *The Logic of Personal Knowledge*, pp. 191-205), "Tacit Knowing and the Pre-Reflective

Cogito," in *Intellect and Hope*, pp. 53-54, and "Hobbes and the Modern Mind," in *The Anatomy of Knowledge*, pp. 14-15.

67. A thoroughgoing articulation of the ontology of emergence is lacking in Polanyi's writings to date. What he has expressed, however, at least provides a basis for a reasonable validity to the understanding of the dimensions of being. It has, as Marjorie Grene points out in *The Knower and the Known* (pp. 224-225), a historical antecedent in Aristotle, though his form-matter theory cannot adequately comprehend the radical innovations of real emergence. Polanyi's conception of the logic of emergence, therefore, could be complemented by something like Whitehead's systematic metaphysics as expressed in *Process and Reality* or a reformulation of Aristotle's categories as expressed in Lonergan's *Insight* (pp. 431-487). Since they would take us too far afield, neither of these possibilities will be pursued here.

68. See "On the Introduction of Science into Moral Subjects," 203-204 and "Faith and Reason," 242.

69. *The Study of Man*, pp. 82-83.

70. "Knowing and Being," p. 134.

71. *The Tacit Dimension*, p. 52.

72. "Life's Irreducible Structure," p. 238.

73. Grene, "Tacit Knowing and the Pre-Reflective Cogito," p. 54.

74. *The Tacit Dimension*, p. 89.

75. *Ibid.*

76. Edward Pols makes a similar clarification, though with different emphases. See his article, "Polanyi and the Problem of Metaphysical Knowledge," in *Intellect and Hope*, pp. 75-80.

77. See, for example, *Science, Faith and Society*, pp. 23, 35; *Personal Knowledge*, p. 311; "The Creative Imagination," 92-93; and *The Tacit Dimension*, pp. 25, 87.

78. See *Science, Faith and Society*, p. 10; *Personal Knowledge*, p. 311; *The Tacit Dimension*, pp. 68, 82; "Problem Solving," 101; and "The Creative Imagination," 88.

79. See section B above, "The Meaning of Reality," especially pp. 109-110.

80. *The Knower and the Known*, p. 222.

81. See Polanyi, "What Is a Painting?" *American Scholar*, XXXIX (1970), 655-669. Even though Polanyi is not directly concerned with clarifying his definition of reality

(sense four), by attempting to explain the reality of a painting as evoking in us an experience that transcends nature (see especially pp. 665-667), he indirectly supports Grene's earlier interpretation of this criterion with respect to art.

82. See *Science, Faith and Society*, pp. 10, 23; *Personal Knowledge*, pp. 146-148; "The Creative Imagination," 86; and Marjorie Grene, *The Knower and the Known*, p. 220.

83. See above, p. 11, n. 7; the reference is to *Personal Knowledge*, p. 304f.

84. *Personal Knowledge*, p. 254.

85. *Ibid.*

86. A strikingly similar critique of this theory as it is espoused in much of contemporary British philosophy is presented by C. B. Daly, "Metaphysics and the Limits of Language," in *New Essays on Religious Language*, ed. by Dallas M. High (New York: Oxford University Press, 1969), p. 123.

87. See *Personal Knowledge*, pp. 71, 104, and 254-255.

88. For contemporary expressions of this traditional understanding of truth, see Karl Rahner, *Spirit in the World*, p. 129 and Bernard Lonergan, *Insight*, p. 552.

89. Pols, "Polanyi and the Problem of Metaphysical Knowledge," pp. 62-63.

90. For this mode of expression see Langdon Gilkey, *Naming the Whirlwind* (Indianapolis: The Bobbs-Merrill Company, Inc., 1969), pp. 296-414; *Religion and the Scientific Future* (New York: Harper & Row, Publishers, 1970), pp. 47-64; and "Empirical Science and Theological Knowing," in *Foundations of Theology*, ed. by Philip McShane (Notre Dame: University of Notre Dame Press, 1972), pp. 93-97. Much of the subsequent analysis in the remainder of this chapter is dependent on these penetrating studies.

91. *Science, Faith and Society*, p. 24.

92. "The Creative Imagination," 88.

93. *The Tacit Dimension*, p. 23.

94. Edward Pols, in his otherwise excellent assessment of Polanyi's thought in relation to our knowledge of the real, does not admit this. He appreciates, for example, how Polanyi's notion of a tacit foreknowledge offers "a self-evidential base for our knowledge" (or, as we are expressing it, an experience of the dimension of ultimacy in our knowledge), but only with respect to the pursuit of scientific truth and not for comprehensive entities in general. As we shall try to demonstrate, it is our contention that he is mistaken in this restrictive

interpretation. See his "Polanyi and the Problem of Metaphysical Knowledge," p. 84, n. 27.

95. "Faith and Reason," 243.

96. "Knowing and Being," p. 129. It is instructive to note that in this article Polanyi begins with an analysis of our acts of tacit knowledge in general, including the recognition of the foreknowledge required for our ability to use general terms, and only then moves to an analysis of the foreknowledge which is manifested in the recognition of a problem. The logical structure of the argument itself is further evidence for the general applicability of this theme.

97. *The Tacit Dimension*, p. 33.

98. This feature of Polanyi's thought finds a strong parallel in Karl Rahner's notion of man's pre-apprehension of being (*Vorgriff ad esse*) which is unthematically co-affirmed as the transcendental condition for the possibility of every thematic affirmation or judgment. See his *Spirit in the World*, Part II, Chapter III, pp. 117-236.

99. *Personal Knowledge*, p. 308.

100. *Ibid.*, pp. 309-310.

101. *Science, Faith and Society*, p. 54.

102. See "The Logic of Tacit Inference," p. 156.

103. *Personal Knowledge*, p. 307.

104. *The Tacit Dimension*, p. 87.

105. *Personal Knowledge*, p. 320. A slightly more nuanced expression of this dimension of ultimacy is presented by Bernard Lonergan in his analysis of the grasp of a prospective judgment as virtually unconditioned. See *Insight*, p. 280.

106. See *Personal Knowledge*, pp. 132-202.

107. *Ibid.*, p. 159.

108. See *The Study of Man*, p. 84 and "The Creative Imagination," 91-92.

109. See *Personal Knowledge*, pp. 321-324 and *The Tacit Dimension*, p. 79.

110. "The Logic of Tacit Inference," p. 141.

111. *The Tacit Dimension*, p. 32.

112. "Tacit Knowing: Its Bearing on Some Problems of Philosophy," p. 168.

154

113. *Personal Knowledge*, p. 317.

114. For a more detailed discussion of mystery in the sense we are using it here, see Karl Rahner, "The Concept of Mystery in Catholic Theology," in *Theological Investigations*, IV (Baltimore: Helicon Press, 1966), pp. 36-73; Bernard Lonergan, *Insight*, pp. 531-549; and John Dunne, *A Search for God in Time and Memory* (New York: The Macmillan Company, 1967), p. 7.

115. *Personal Knowledge*, p. 324.

116. *The Tacit Dimension*, p. 92 and *Personal Knowledge*, p. 405.

CHAPTER V

A FOUNDATIONAL INQUIRY INTO THE STRUCTURE

OF RELIGIOUS BELIEF

A. The Continuity between Faith and Reason

The goal of this inquiry has been to propose a general
conception of human knowledge which would provide a foundational analysis explanatory of all intellectual activity, including
religious belief. The success of this endeavor thus has been
dependent on a fundamental assumption. In order that the goal
be achieved, we have had to presuppose an underlying harmony
or continuity, in some sense, between religious faith and other
human intellectual enterprises. This sort of assumption is not
universally accepted, and the ranks of those who do not accept
it include believers as well as non-believers. Consequently a
brief analysis of this problem is in order so that the meaning
and validity of our assumptions may be clarified.

The relationship between faith and reason is a perennial
problem for religious thought.[1] This is not at all surprising
in view of the historicity of cultural frameworks. The problem becomes particularly acute, however, during those transi-
tional periods between the gradual erosion of the authority of
a fading cultural *Gestalt* and the emergence of the competing
attraction of its still dimly perceived successor. At such
times the fundamental conceptions of reality which dominate
the age are called into question, and all previous responses
to this problem must be re-examined.

While any response will necessarily have qualifying elements derived from the particular cultural setting in which
the question is raised, the solutions logically possible may
be categorized according to three general positions.[2] One

tendency holds that in some sense faith and reason are harmonious, or reconcilable, or complementary. A second tendency would understand the acceptance of one term to imply the renunciation of the other. This category comprises two opposing poles: on the one hand a fideist view which accepts the demands of faith, usually understood in a fundamentalist or literalist sense, at the expense of reason; and on the other hand a rationalist view which follows the dictates of reason, usually understood in a completely autonomous sense, and rejects anything not contained under this rubric, especially religious belief. Here the problem is solved by denying the validity of one element which causes the problem. A third tendency maintains that faith and reason are the subjects of distinct spheres or realms, that there is no continuity between the two, but that both are valid in their proper areas. According to this view the problem is resolved by arguing that there is no problem or that the problem arises only when one intrudes upon the domain of the other.

In terms of the structural elements which constitute human intellectual activity at the foundational level disclosed by our analysis, only the first of these possibilities can be convincingly upheld.

Insofar as the second tendency is concerned, the basis for this judgment consists in the recognition that any concept functions within a given intellectual horizon. "Faith" and "reason" are no exceptions. Therefore any explicit conceptions of the meaning of faith and reason are derived partially from the prevailing cultural horizon which provides the most general notions of reality tacitly assumed by the age. Since the cultural horizon, within which the particular conceptions of faith and reason are formed, is normally not noticed, it is quite possible for some groups within the culture to misapprehend the reality of faith or reason by conceiving them in isolation from other elements of the cultural framework or by absolutizing them in a way which tries to make the conceptions directly equivalent to the reality. From such a limited perspective, faith and reason may indeed appear to be contradictory. The antagonism, however, is the result of a failure to probe deeply enough into the realities involved from within the given perspective. Whitehead has expressed this point in his own inimitable manner: "You cannot shelter theology from science, or science from theology; nor can you shelter either of them from metaphysics, or metaphysics from either of them. There is no short cut to truth."[3] Any attempt to safeguard "faith" by a deliberate limitation and refusal to encounter the truth of other elements of a culture which would force faith and reason into competing and antagonistic positions is bound to truncate and falsify its reality.

The third tendency, even though it is much more sophisticated than the second, is also lacking at the foundational level of inquiry. During the modern period in the West it has been articulated in the characteristic form of a discontinuity between "nature" (or science) and "history" (or revelation). According to this view, then, "nature and history are structures in reality so fundamentally different that it ought to be said they have nothing in common. They are incommensurable. Conflict between them is impossible."[4] The dichotomy here is one of method, where two distinct structures of reality are operative.[5] "History" is that which refers to the question of meaning, particularly the meaning of man, while "nature" is that which refers to the question of things or essences and is silent about man.[6] Historically this dichotomy goes back to the Kantian distinction between speculative and pratical reason.[7] Unfortunately, understanding the relationship between faith and reason in this way carries with it a set of liabilities similar to those which we had uncovered earlier in our study.

The major difficulty in this view can be expressed by considering the following question: In what sense are the two disparate structures of reality related to "reality" (or whatever else one may wish to term the objective referent)? If nature and history are not "two different kinds of reality"[8] and if at the same time they are not "two ways of experiencing some third reality lurking in the background,"[9] then to what does the methodological distinction refer in addition to some formal abstraction? The position seems to assert that the question of meaning, which includes the meaning of faith, is speaking of reality, but only of historical reality within

which faith is discernable. On the other hand, the question of
fact, which is also a structure of reality, has nothing to say
about the meaning of man because it is, of course, non-histori-
cal and constituted by the realm of nature. This is very difficult to maintain consistently because in those cases where a
fact from the realm of nature may speak of the meaning of man
--as a theory of evolution would seem to be able to do--it must
then be suddenly transposed from the realm of nature into the
realm of history.[10]

It would appear that there is a fundamental ambiguity
here concerning man's knowledge of reality. If, through faith,
a person knows that "God created man," then this must have
something to say about nature and the fact of evolution. Similarly, if a person knows that it is a fact of nature that man
evolved, then this has some light to shed on the meaning of
"God created man." Any recognition of a mutual interdependence
of this sort implies the further question that asks how "nature" and "history" can be thus related. To point out that man
can look at the same reality (not a third reality) in two different ways is to demand an explanation of how man does this.
Again, at this foundational level the third view of the relationship between faith and reason does not probe deeply enough.

Even though the view which holds faith and reason to be
dichotomous has been found incomplete, it nevertheless does
provide a valid correction of the second tendency. This probably accounts for much of its attractiveness among its adherents.[11] It does not make the mistake of expecting faith to
tell us everything about the world, nor does it expect science
to explain everything about the meaning of man. The context
within which certain issues are raised determines the focus of
the issues and the scope of the answers. By clearly separating
the two concerns, it constantly warns against expecting a type
of answer from an approach to reality which precludes the answer. This insight must be taken into account in our attempt
to explain the continuity between faith and reason.

When these introductory clarifications are taken into
the context of Polanyi's analysis of human knowing, then it
should be clear that the proposal for understanding the continuity between faith and reason will not be dependent simply on

some explicit conceptualization of faith and reason, nor will
it result primarily from some overlapping of a commonly shared
object of concern. Rather, their relationship can be seen to
lie at the fundamental level of the structure of human intellectual inquiry. From this underlying level of human consciousness every search for the meaning of reality springs. Upon this
basis particular conceptions of reason and faith emerge and only
in conjunction with these conceptions are specific realms of reality demarcated.

The significant feature of this proposal is its understanding of knowing as a heuristic achievement. From the fundamental structures sustaining this effort, the specific ways
of knowing which arise form a continuum. At every point on
this continuum there is a combination of a personal appropriation of some specific framework and the personal utilization of
this framework to extend one's comprehension of the real. Expressed in terms of the structure of tacit knowledge, this
means that every act of knowing comprises a tacit reliance on
the authority embodied in a specific intellectual tradition in
order to focus on some aspect of reality. At this level of
analysis, all our knowledge exhibits a similar structure. It
is operative whether we are trying to analyze some chemical
property or to account for some historical event.[12]

From the vantage point of this dynamic structure of knowing, then, the various fields of knowledge with their proper
methodologies and areas of concern do not differ in kind. The
same fundamental structure sustains them all. Nevertheless,
there are differences in the explicit ways this structure is
actualized. The theory of tacit knowing accounts for these
differences according to the degree of participation of the
knower in that which he knows. Once the various realms of inquiry are understood to be activated by the same dynamic structure of knowing, then the differences between them become differences only of degree.[13]

These considerations can now be amplified by recalling
the similarity in the structure of our knowing a physical object and another person and by observing the transition between
them. We know a physical object, such as a book, by dwelling
in an intellectual framework which allows us to relate to it

intentionally and by incorporating its particulars so that we may comprehend it focally. As we move to a knowledge of realities on a higher level of existence there is a parallel growth in intellectual frameworks and degree of incorporation of the particulars of the thing known. In order to know a machine, therefore, we must dwell in a horizon capable of appreciating its operational principles and must incorporate its particulars so that we may tacitly integrate them into their coherent whole. When we know a living thing, we must pass over to a horizon capable of dealing with life by permitting us to make the integration of its particulars at this more profound level. Similarly the recognition of a person requires the further reliance on a framework which includes the operations of intelligence. And, again, if we wish to recognize the moral responsibility of a person we must move to an even higher level of indwelling. Polanyi has summarized this process by remarking

> . . .that the participation of the knower in the thing he knows increases steadily as the objects of knowledge ascend to ever higher levels of existence, and that, correspondingly, the observer also applies ever higher standards of appreciation to the things known by him. These two trends will combine to an ever more ample and more equal sharing of existence between the knower and the known, so that when we reach the point at which one man knows another man, the knower so fully dwells in that which he knows, that we can no longer place the two on different logical levels. This is to say that when we arrive at the contemplation of a human being as a responsible person, and we apply to him the same standards as we accept for ourselves, our knowledge of him has definitely lost the character of an observation and has become an encounter instead.[14]

Because all knowing unfolds through such increasingly progressive degrees of indwelling corresponding to the level of reality being known, it is impossible to make any absolute demarcation between faith and reason. This is so on the side of the knower where we find a continuity of specific ways of knowing: "From the minimum of indwelling exercised in a physical observation, we move without a break to the maximum of indwelling which is a total commitment."[15] This is also the case from the side of reality which discloses a hierarchy of levels of emergence leading to the question of the significance of this cosmic panorama: "Thus natural knowing expands continuously into the knowledge of the supernatural."[16]

Nothing that has been expressed so far on the continuity between faith and reason should be taken as detracting from the distinctiveness of faith. What we have stressed to this point has been the human mode of apprehension which remains constant throughout. But the degree of indwelling varies. Since any form of indwelling affects our way of being in the world, religious indwelling, which demands a radical commitment, modifies what we are as persons in a way no lesser form of indwelling can possible approximate.[17] An explanation of this characteristic now requires an understanding of the dynamics proper to religious faith.

B. *Religious Faith as "Breaking Out"*

1. The experience of the sacred and the human mode of knowing

The problem of understanding religious faith has many facets and may be approached from various perspectives. It may be understood quite properly according to the requirements demanded by some specific theological or doctrinal position, which could bring up again the problem of the relationship between faith and reason. An appeal to such a stance at this point would thus not be beneficial, because our inquiry is attempting to establish the general conditions for recognizing the validity of religious faith. From the vantage of the requirements necessitated by our foundational inquiry, this program can be successful only by explaining the processes which constitute the act of faith. Such an explanation consists in exposing those elements uncovered by our analysis of human cognitional activity which permit us to raise the question of ultimate meaning. Therefore our task here is to extrapolate from the structure of human conscious activity, which has been derived from our interpretation of Polanyi's theory of tacit knowing, an explanation of that which occurs whenever man attempts to respond to ultimate questions.

When the problem of our knowledge of reality was probed through an analysis of our cognitional activity on the foundational level at the conclusion of the previous chapter, an experience of the dimension of ultimacy was disclosed to be an integral constituent. This dimension is experienced not as an object of our comprehension in the sense of a knowledge of some specific entity, but as a qualifying condition enabling us to affirm the truth of anything at all. It is known only by way of a tacit foreknowledge which engages our heuristic strivings by means of our dwelling in an articulate framework.

From the vantage point of the structure of human knowing disclosed by this foundational inquiry, all men are open to the transcendent source of this experience of ultimacy. Because of this orientation to the dimension of ultimacy, all men can come to a provisional knowledge of the reality of specific comprehensive entities and can make judgments about them. In this primordial sense, then, all men are religious.

This designation of man as religious obviously goes beyond the usual meaning ascribed to the term. It should nevertheless be clear that the sense intended here refers to man's fundamental way of being in the world, and not to any specific way he may or may not actualize this capability for experiencing the dimension of the ultimate. The recognition that man's constitution as a conscious being is grounded in an experience which transcends particular judgments is in fact nothing more than a further specification of the meaning of man described earlier.[18] Insofar as man constitutes himself in history by being drawn to an ever more comprehensive discovery of reality, the possibility of experiencing the sacred is always present to the individual person. The assertion that man is religious is thus justified in terms of our foundational analysis because the dimension of ultimacy, through which man transcends the world of contingent events, sustains every act of comprehending the real.

Moreover, the study of the religious phenomenon itself justifies this usage. In any concrete historical religious tradition, the sacred, no matter how it is conceived, is that which is real in the ultimate sense and that from which all other actions and entities derive their meaning and reality. Mircea Eliade has described this feature of the religious phenomenon as follows:

> . . .the sacred is pre-eminently the *real*, at once

> power, efficacity, the source of life and fecundity.
> Religious man's desire to live *in the sacred* is in
> fact equivalent to his desire to take up his abode
> in objective reality, not to let himself be para-
> lyzed by the never-ceasing relativity of purely
> subjective experiences, to live in a real and ef-
> fective world, and not an illusion. This behavior
> is documented on every plane of religious man's
> existence. . .[19]

The data from the religious phenomenon itself thus converge
with the analysis of human cognitional activity.

These observations now permit an explanation of the structure operative in the human mode of knowing, seen from the
foundational level of inquiry, when a person encounters, or
claims to encounter, the sacred. According to the theory of
tacit knowing, the knower comprehends the known by dwelling in
a framework which allows him to integrate its particulars into
a coherent whole. In order to comprehend a reality on a higher
level of existence, he must progress to a correspondingly deeper
level of indwelling. Throughout this continuum the tacit reliance on reality as such is always present, grounding all historically conditioned horizons and pervading all heuristic
thrusts beyond them. As a result the possibility of questioning the meaning and significance of reality itself is likewise
always present through our tacit foreknowledge. Whenever this
dimension becomes the focus of anyone's faith and hope, or
doubt and despair, this person is engaged in an encounter with
the transcendent fullness or the unfathomable depths of the
sacred.

In this context, then, religious faith is to be understood
as that form of indwelling which has as its primary goal the
breaking out toward the transcendent source of the experience
of ultimacy.[20] It strives to break out of the limited horizons
which any form of indwelling imposes in order to contemplate
directly that which is experienced tacitly in ordinary acts of
knowledge as the dimension of ultimacy. This ability of our
cognitional powers to break out of a limited horizon and to
contemplate the real is the structure of religious belief insofar as it can be explained from the vantage point of our foundational inquiry.

This explanation can be amplified somewhat by a consideration of a primary and authentic expression of religious

belief--mystical encounter. Insofar as can be ascertained from the claims of mystics themselves, the constitutive feature of the mystical experience is the feeling of an immediate presence of a reality transcending the world.[21] Any concrete description of this experience, of course, will vary according to the different forms of indwelling from which the mystic begins. So whether the effect of the experience is understood as an absorption or a personal totalization, or whether the source of the experience is interpreted as a positive fullness or as a tranquil no-thing, it is always identical in this characteristic of presence.

From the vantage point of the theory of tacit knowing, Polanyi has made the following instructive observations of mystical experience:

> The religious mystic achieves contemplative communion as a result of an elaborate effort of thought, supported by ritual. By concentrating on the presence of God, who is beyond all physical appearances, the mystic seeks to relax the intellectual control which his powers of perception instinctively exercise over the scene confronting them. His fixed gaze no longer scans each object in its turn and his mind ceases to identify their particulars. The whole framework of intelligent understanding, by which he normally appraises his impressions, sinks into abeyance and uncovers a world experienced uncomprehendingly as a divine miracle . . . [The mystical tradition] invites us, through a succession of "detachments", to seek in absolute ignorance union with Him who is beyond all being and all knowledge. We see things then not focally, but as part of a cosmos, as features of God.[22]

Expressed more technically we could say that the mystic's focal awareness converges toward the tacit ground of his foreknowledge of the real, bypassing the mediation of some limited horizon. In this state the objects of the world, normally comprehended through a tacit reliance on the foreknowledge of the real, are known subsidiarily by being taken up into a higher level of integration.

A consequence, which flows immediately from this consideration of the limiting case of religious mysticism, is that the structure of religious belief, insofar as it is approached from the vantage point of the dynamics of human knowing, results in a negative prehension. This means that, in addition to explaining how the human mind unfolds through a tacit reliance on a dimension of ultimacy, our foundational analysis does not provide any positive signification which clarifies the nature of this dimension. Of course, one might attempt to argue from the principles outlined in the previous chapter on the logic of emergence that, just as an entity can only be understood by integrating its constitutive elements and focusing on its highest level of existence, so also the sacred can only be understood as that which provides the meaning of emergence and human life by serving as their ultimate level of organization. Unfortunately, this presupposes that the dimension of ultimacy refers us toward that which does in fact supply this sort of meaning--a presupposition not demanded by the analysis of human knowing itself. On the contrary, it would be just as plausible to argue, if one were to depend solely on the foundational inquiry into human knowing, that the experience of the dimension of ultimacy, which breaks down our familiar forms of meaning, thrusts us into the presence of nothingness.[23] By focusing on its disjointed particulars instead of its comprehensive features, this view would maintain that the only meaning the universe possesses is the provisional one we supply to it, because both the world and man are absurd when considered by themselves. This view, however, in addition to assuming that no higher integration can be made, carries within itself a further set of of liabilities which have already been exposed in the treatment of the personal variant of moral inversion. Thus it follows that if we attempt to interpret the significance of our ability to break out solely from the results of the foundational analysis of human cognitional activity, both theism and atheism are possible.

The reason why any attempt to move from a knowledge of the world to an understanding of the sacred should result in a formal ignorance can be explained by reviewing the dynamics of human knowing in the encounter with the sacred. Insofar as the tacit foreknowledge of the real provides the ultimate ground for all our concrete judgments, the real in itself cannot function by becoming an object of comprehension. Assuming then that in the act of religious faith the believer breaks out toward the transcendent source of this dimension of ultimacy and experiences it as the sacred, he can never have a "knowledge" of the sacred in the technical sense of comprehending an entity in light of some framework. In other words, we always know a particular thing as an aspect of reality, or a level of reality, or a degree of reality because we dwell in a framework whose ultimate horizon is reality as such; since our reliance on this horizon, which is experienced as a dimension of ultimacy, is precisely that which makes comprehension possible, we can know it only by a tacit foreknowledge and never through a focal comprehension.[24]

The same conclusion can be drawn from an examination of the way in which the concepts of "existence" or "reality" function within a conceptual system, and then generalizing this to any conceptualization of the sacred within a given conceptual system. Whenever the concept of "existence" is used, we do not know *what* we intend. This is to say that "existence" is never an object of comprehension; it is always the presupposition functioning tacitly by allowing us to use our conceptual systems to make existential judgments. "Existence" or "reality" is the context in which our judgments are made. Their meaning is experienced tacitly as the ontological aspect in our knowing some thing, not as the content of any act of knowledge. They are not intelligible concepts because they are non-comprehendable. Insofar as we have been arguing that religious faith concerns itself with this dimension, it would follow that our conceptual system does not permit us to comprehend the sacred. The reason for this is that the intelligibility and communicability of human knowledge presupposes a conceptual system and an object of experience which it can inform. Thus every conceptual system devised by man is limited to the world as the only commonly shared object of experience. Since the sacred transcends the world of our experience, no attempt to comprehend the sacred by informing it in light of a conceptual system can succeed. This is so even in the limiting case of mysticism, which was implied by Polanyi's description of the state as opening the mystic to "a world experienced uncomprehendingly as a divine miracle."[25] Even if we accepted the validity of a mystic's experience, he still could not provide an intelligible account of his experience by relying on a conceptual system

devised to comprehend the world--except perhaps to those who
shared his experience.[26]

This is not, however, the whole of the matter. So far our
analysis has exposed the dynamics of faith exclusively from the
vantage point of the structure of the human mode of knowing.
On this level of inquiry faith appears as that form of indwelling which breaks out toward the dimension of the ultimate. The
only understanding provided by this analysis is an explanation
of the operation of human cognitional activity which functions
during the performance of the act of faith. The "content" of
faith remains unknown. Nevertheless religious believers do
make cognitive claims about the dimension of the sacred and occasionally derivative claims about the intelligibility of the
world. The problem of understanding its capacity for making
such claims must now be analyzed from an expanded vantage point
which includes faith itself.

2. Conditions for the recognition of the sacred

Our reflections have led to a preliminary understanding of
religious belief insofar as an intelligible account of its dynamics was exposed in terms of the structure of human cognition.
At this foundational level we understood a religious believer
to be a person who adopts a mode of being in the world which
enables him to break out of his normal patterns of indwelling
toward that dimension which permeates and sustains all his cognitive endeavors. In breaking out toward this "object," he
recognizes the sacred. Since the human knower cannot comprehend this object by means of a reliance on an intellectual
framework, the further problem arises here which consists in
explaining under what conditions such a recognition of the sacred can occur. This analysis is required so that some account
may be given for the cognitive claims made by religious believers.

One of the pervasive constituents of human knowing uncovered by this inquiry is that every intelligible affirmation of
reality unfolds by means of a tacit reliance on an antecedent
intellectual framework. These horizons enable man to expand
his intellectual control beyond his immediate perceptions
through a reliance on the accumulated insights of past genera-

tions. By submitting himself to them and learning to appreciate their validity, he makes himself in history by acting in accordance with their norms of intelligibility. Through such historical indwelling, moreover, he can then alter or expand the limits of his inherited horizons because of his own personal responsibility validating such existential choices in the encounter with the dimension of ultimacy. We have already seen how this mutual interdependence between a historically conditioned framework and man's personal striving to know the real permits us to admit the contingency of individual judgments and the development of human knowledge, while at the same time to uphold our claims to the truth.

Since man is such a historical being, this implies that, if he is to discover any ultimate meaning for reality, he must become open to and aware of the possibility of the presence of the sacred in history. If there is to be an understanding of the sacred in any sense, this is a primary condition for it which derives from our analysis of the human mode of knowing in the context of the sacred. Because man cannot intelligibly comprehend reality as such through his own creative intellectual powers, only a possible manifestation from the side of the sacred itself can provide this kind of intelligibility. On the other hand, because man's cognitive powers which are grounded in the dimension of ultimacy show that he is in fact ordered toward reality in its most profound sense, such a possible manifestation of the sacred could be recognized by man.[27] Thus even though men are religious in the primordial sense discussed above, this analysis of the implication of man's orientation in history explains that man can recognize the sacred only if he acknowledges his responsibility in the face of the ultimate.

This observation maintains only that man can and ought to become aware of any manifestation of the sacred. It simply demonstrates the real possibility of a necessary condition, derived from our analysis of the human mode of knowing, which describes how the sacred could be the object of a cognitive experience by man. The actual occurrence of any disclosure on the part of the sacred, however, can be determined only concretely. Therefore a second condition for recognizing the sacred is that man must learn to perceive the sacred.

This is, of course, a condition required for the perception of any reality. Fundamentally it implies that a person must accept a particular framework in order to understand any reality the framework claims to enlighten. Such submission to the authority of an intellectual horizon is the context providing the conditions for our intelligent activity and is a constitutive feature of the theory of personal knowledge. "Tacit assent and intellectual passions, the sharing of an idiom and of a cultural heritage, affiliation to a like-minded community: such are the impulses which shape our vision of the nature of things on which we rely for our mastery of things. No intelligence, however critical or organized, can operate outside such a fiduciary framework."[28] The intelligibility of any articulate affirmations, in other words, can be appreciated only by sharing the standpoint in which they are uttered.

This points to the significance of Polanyi's emphasis on St. Augustine's maxim, *nisi credideritis, non intelligitis,* particularly in its application to the intelligibility of religious belief. Augustine's contention that an understanding of the mystery of the sacred requires an antecedent belief in it is one of the recurrent themes in his writings:

> . . .unless we had first to believe the great and divine thing which we desire to understand, the Prophet would not have spoken idly when he said, "Unless you believe, you shall not understand" (Is. vii, 9, *sec*. LXX). Our Lord himself, too, by His words and deeds exhorted those whom He called to salvation, that they first believe. But afterwards, when He was talking of the gift of which He would give to believers, did not say, "this is eternal life, that they may believe," but "this is eternal life: that they may know Thee, the only true God, and Jesus Christ whom Thou hast sent" (John xvii, 3). Furthermore He said to those who were already believers, "Seek and you shall find" (Matt. vii, 7). For what is believed to be unknown cannot be called found, nor is anyone capable of finding God, unless he first believe that he will eventually find Him. . .That which we seek on His exhortation, we shall find by His showing it to us, so far as it is possible to such as us to find this in this life.[29]

Our analysis is thus reminiscent of Augustine's reflections where an understanding of the sacred is conditioned by the ability to perceive it which comes only by an acceptance of its standpoint.

Lest this be misconstrued as an appeal to a blind author-
itarianism, however, it must be recalled that the experience of
ultimacy accompanying our reliance on any framework continues
to function. Whenever we wish to explore the meaning of any
reality, a mutual interaction operates between the object under
consideration and the framework through which we consider the
object. A more penetrating discovery of the meaning of the
reality may lead to an alteration in our framework either by
increasing our conviction of its validity, or by modifying certain elements which are now seen to be incomplete, or even by
the rejection of it and the acceptance of a new horizon for
understanding the reality in question.[30] Augustine himself
admits this dialectic when he acknowledges that the recognition
of truth is a criterion for accepting any belief.[31] The need
for accepting a manifestation of the sacred places no restrictions on human knowing; on the contrary, it supplies a condition through which any intelligibility it may possess can be
recognized.

Since any intellectual framework will normally be embodied
concretely in the social community which espouses it, the conditions for recognizing the sacred outlined so far can be actualized by an individual person only if he opens himself to
the guidance of a specific religious tradition. To do so requires an existential choice which will affect radically his
manner of being in the world. But the choice is not arbitrary.
The person is seeking after an understanding of the dimension
of ultimacy toward which he finds himself directed. This effort places him at a threshold similar to the state experienced
during all creative breakthroughs. It has been described by
Polanyi as follows:

> His quest transforms him by compelling him to
> make a sequence of choices. Does this mean that he
> is existentially choosing himself? In a sense it
> does; he does seek intellectual growth. But he does
> *not* sit back and choose at his pleasure a new exis-
> tence. He strains his imagination to the utmost
> to find a path that might lead to a superior life
> of the mind. All his existential choices are made
> in response to a potential discovery; they consist
> in sensing and following a gradient of understand-
> ing which will lead to the expansion of his mental

existence. Every step is an effort to meet an immediate necessity; his freedom is continuous service.[32]

The beginning of the understanding of the sacred, therefore, is a conversion--no matter how tentative or hesitant its initial status may be.

In order for such a conversion to occur, however, an appreciation of a final condition for the recognition of the sacred is required. The usual way in which the meaning of an unknown reality is brought to anyone's attention is through some form of communication. If man is to be aware of a possible manifestation of the sacred in history, and if he searches for it through an acceptance of the proclamation of a religious community, then clearly one of the primary instruments for achieving this understanding will be language. We have already seen, though, that the conceptual systems devised by man can never circumscribe the ultimate. Therefore religious language can be understood only on the condition that one recognizes that it conveys its meaning through symbolic or analogical modes of expression.

A failure to recognize this characteristic will lead inevitably to a reduction of religious language to the level of vacuous utterances. A comparison of the structural elements of faith and the semantic aspect of tacit knowing clarifies why this is so. In our normal knowledge of the world, the "data" we experience are made intelligible because we integrate them into meaningful wholes by relying tacitly on our conceptual systems. These systems are thus created by man to inform and to convey the meaning of his experiences. The conceptual systems themselves are tacitly experienced to be valid (or invalid) because of our reliance on them for making concrete affirmations through which we experience further the dimension of the ultimate as the condition upholding their application. This means then that they supply a narrower frame of reference than the sacred itself. As a result the intelligibility we supply to the world through our conceptual systems cannot be used legitimately to "comprehend" the sacred by a univocal extension of meaning.

Since faith nevertheless does claim to lead to an "understanding" of the sacred, religious language must provide some meaning. The source of its intelligibility, however, cannot be man. Religious faith, we have argued, is a form of indwelling which has as its primary function a breaking out toward the sacred. To the extent that a believer achieves this, he transcends the normal bounds of intelligibility and is supplied with another source of intelligibility--the light of faith produced by the encounter with the sacred. The words he now uses are infused with an additional meaning because of their reference to the sacred.[33]

For this reason religious language, since it necessarily relies on the meaning derived from the conceptual systems embodied in any historical culture, cannot be taken to intend precisely the same thing that the terms it uses intend when they function normally to inform our experience of the world. In their secular use, the terms enable us to comprehend an aspect of reality because we can affirm it through the meaning provided by our tacit reliance on the conceptual system in which the terms function. In their religious context the language functions primarily by engaging the believer in the attempt to break out. *What* is intended in a religious utterance goes beyond the norms of intelligibility provided by the conceptual system. As a result the language of faith does not comprehend its object. The "understanding" that comes from religious belief is thus fundamentally proleptic, because the meaning faith supplies is causal in the sense that it draws the believer into an ever greater communion with the sacred.

The meaning of faith, then, is recognized by dwelling in the heuristic vision it sustains.[34] Because of his dwelling in the community of faith which is the bearer of a manifestation of the sacred, the believer is enabled to recognize the sacred through an act of worship rather than as the comprehended content of an affirmation.[35] Insofar as faith is an indwelling fostering a breaking out, its expressions of worship are properly speaking neither true nor false. The attempt to break out can only be genuine or hypocritical. Since, from this perspective, religious faith does not make factual assertions, its language is symbolic "precisely because the symbol does not only signify the thing intended but also embodies its presence and calls upon the hearer to enter the world which the symbol reveals."[36] Like all heuristic visions, including science and the arts, its meaning can only be held tacitly through an appreciation of its validity derived from experiencing it.[37]

The general implications of our explanation of religious belief as a breaking out show that a recognition of the sacred is always a gift bestowed by the sacred. At the same time the recognition of this manifestation of the sacred requires a concomitant response on the part of man that is a total transformation. Only consequent upon such a commitment to the object toward which he is striving does his new form of indwelling become meaningful.

Our analysis so far has attempted to provide an explanation for the validity of the act of faith and the status of its cognitive claims from the perspective of the structure of religious belief as a form of indwelling. In addition to this general theoretical explication, however, we must recognize that a specific religious experience will assume a concrete form which has implications beyond the inculcation of its heuristic vision. Accordingly a religious experience, in addition to breaking out toward the sacred, will be conditioned by the events through which it occurs and the cultural framework in which it is cast. Certain of these events and interpretations become privileged by providing an articulate set of guidelines for fostering the attempt at breaking out. Even though in the religious context they are symbolic and point beyond themselves toward the sacred, they nevertheless constitute a collection of "data" which serve as a basis for understanding the implications of faith in the world. In this sense religious belief can be fostered or impaired by the understanding of empirical evidence which corroborates or contradicts the data sustaining its heuristic vision. To explain how such claims affect the meaning of religious indwelling requires now an examination of theological understanding.

C. *Theology as Understanding*

Through our foundational inquiry into the structure of human knowing we have been able to offer an explanation for the possibility and meaningfulness of religious belief. Because of the experience of the dimension of ultimacy sustaining all our efforts to comprehend reality, we can submit ourselves to a form of indwelling which strives to enlighten this dimension. If we do, the meaning of the sacred is discovered by breaking out toward it. In this sense religious belief is a heuristic vision whose meaning is known tacitly by dwelling in it. In addition to this, however, the tradition which embodies this indwelling derives from special experiences and expresses symbolically the heuristic vision it fosters. Its primary meaning is thus embedded in claims with empirical and historical aspects. The task of analyzing these claims and explaining how they contribute to an understanding of the implications of the primary meaning of the religious tradition is the role of theology.

An explanation of theological understanding is a complex task because these several interconnected levels of meaning are involved. In terms of our foundational analysis, the primary source of meaning for theological understanding is derived from the encounter with the sacred experienced in breaking out. Yet theology expresses this meaning through assertions about specific facts, by means of interpretations of historical events, and in terms of culturally conditioned frameworks--all of which have other meanings besides their reference to the sacred. Our attempt to explain the understanding which theological inquiry achieves will consist in outlining schematically the relationship between these various levels of meaning. Since theology proper can be done only in a specific context, we shall refer to examples drawn from Christian thought whenever we wish to illustrate a general principle.

Our analysis of the structure of religious belief has shown that the fundamental presupposition of any theological inquiry is the dwelling in a religious tradition or, at the very least, an openness to such an indwelling. Unless theological expressions are seen to be disclosing the implications of the heuristic vision sustaining them, the understanding provided by theology will appear meaningless or even self-contradictory.[38] Any attempt to understand theology outside this framework of meaning is bound to fail because such an attempt would judge the validity of theological claims solely from the world circumscribed by observable experience which cannot comprehend its meaning. The specifically religious import of any theological statement cannot be understood except by those who share the form of indwelling it is attempting to clarify. In this sense, "theology reveals, or tries to reveal, the implications of religious worship, and it can be said to be true or false, but only as regards its adequacy in formulating and purifying a pre-existing religious faith."[39]

Herein lies the objectivity of theological understanding. Theology is objective not in the sense of the impersonal detachment which we have already found to be inadequate, but in the sense that "we must so submit ourselves to the dictates of the object that we think in terms of it, and not in terms of what we think we already know about it."[40] This general methodological principle is applicable to all levels of understanding. Without exercising such a faithfulness to the object of inquiry, all our assertions about it would be nothing more than sheer subjectivism. The "detachment" frequently understood as a requirement of objectivity is nothing more than a negative expression of this principle. It is not any sort of detachment from the object which fosters objectivity; rather it is our faithfulness to the object which permits us to be detached from presuppositions which are discovered to be unwarranted in light of the object.

Theologically, this means that the understanding of the sacred must not be made subservient to scientific premisses, nor to metaphysical systems, nor even to a long-standing theological tradition. Rather, the sacred itself must always be the reality in light of which the adequacy of any approach for understanding its meaning is to be judged. A theologian is capable of expressing the meaning of the sacred, which is derived from his indwelling, only because of his faithfulness to the object experienced through his indwelling. For a Christian theologian, therefore, this would mean that the basis of his attempts to understand the implications of the Christian faith is his faithfulness to the experience of God derived from his dwelling in the community of worship and to the normative proclamation of this meaning, particularly as the Word of God forming this community is recorded in the Bible.

Starting from the giveness and primacy of its object,

theological understanding unfolds through two complementary phases. The first concerns itself with an understanding of the meaning of the tradition as it had been expressed in the past. The second consists in expressing that meaning today through a reliance on the indwelling of faith and in dialogue with contemporary cultural frameworks. Both historical investigation and contemporary exposition derive from and lead back to the meaning recognized in breaking out. In this dual movement various levels of meaning come into play, all of them integrated by the meaning derived from the religious indwelling. We shall examine briefly the relationship between these levels of meaning as they interact in each phase.

In the task of historical analysis, theological understanding comprises at least these levels of meaning: textual criticism, exegesis, historical criticism, and historical theology. Since our understanding of the past is based on surviving records, a preliminary task for theological understanding is establishing what the text is and what the words of the text mean. At these levels the appropriate methods of textual criticism and the principles derived from a knowledge of languages apply. Upon this basis the intention of the text must be interpreted. Here historical research attempts to determine the accuracy of the events to which the documents refer, the significance ascribed to these events by the witnesses, the assumptions of the cultural horizon within which these events are understood, and how these assumptions affected the interpretation afforded these events by the witnesses who dwelled in them. Historical criticism thus analyzes the text in terms of its own self-understanding and in its relationship to the broader cultural spectrum in which it is situated.

Insofar as it is dependent on these levels of meaning, the first phase of theological inquiry functions much like other empirical sciences in that the results of these inquiries serve as data. To this extent, the primary meaning of religious indwelling is dependent on the experience of the world. A believer's recognition of the validity of his religious indwelling thus depends on how well the meaning of its heuristic vision accords with these experiences. This symbiotic relationship between interpretive frameworks and certain empirical events is similar to any other form of indwelling, be it scientific, political, or artistic. It is equally true of religious indwelling because "the universe of every great articulate system is constructed by elaborating and transmuting one particular aspect of anterior experience: The Christian faith elaborates and renders effective the supernatural aspect of anterior experience in terms of its own internal experience."[41] The importance of these levels of meaning thus consists in explaining the anterior experience on which the religious tradition is supposedly based and demonstrating that this experience can in fact support its heuristic vision.

Nevertheless it is clear that these preliminary levels of meaning, while they contribute significant elements to theological understanding, do not, of themselves, "produce" faith. From the vantage point of our analysis, the reason for this is that the most that can be derived from inquiries into these levels of meaning is the recognition of clues which point to something beyond themselves. The religious tradition, for example, may be approached from a perspective which precludes its distinctively religious meaning with the result that the possibility of its religious significance will be discounted beforehand. Much of nineteenth century scholarship, which published successive "lives" of Jesus based on rationalist assumptions, is a well known instance of this fact. In order for the religious level of meaning to be understood, the indwelling of faith must be accepted so that the results of the studies may function as clues illuminating the meaning of the heuristic vision of faith. In its phase of historical analysis, therefore, theological understanding requires the contribution of historical theology to complete its understanding of the distinctively religious meaning of the tradition.

The attempt to understand the various levels of meaning which the first phase of theological inquiry seeks, unfortunately, is complicated by the fact that the persons who are today pursuing these investigations dwell in their own conceptual frameworks. Consequently, before the second phase of theological exposition may begin, a contemporary theological understanding must reflect on the cultural assumptions of its own era. Such reflection will assess the conceptions of know-

ledge and reality presupposed by the age in light of its experience of breaking out. Through this effort a clarification of
theology's self-understanding at the time is exposed along with
its task in the face of standards currently held by the culture.
From these reflections the conditions required both for approach-
ing the historical tradition and for formulating a contemporary
expression of the faith can be set forth.

Our foundational inquiry has been devoted precisely to
this task. Earlier in our analysis of contemporary presuppositions we have tried to explain how our knowledge of reality
can be affirmed even though the explicit forms of our assertions are rooted in historically conditioned frameworks. This
analysis can now be extended to an examination of our ability
to understand theological affirmations made in differing cultural or conceptual contexts.

Expressed in general terms, we can say that a person in-
quiring into the meaning of an aspect of reality as it was perceived through a past cultural framework can come to understand
it because an isomorphic relationship exists between his understanding of reality today and the understanding of reality as
it was perceived through the past framework.[42] This does not
mean that the frameworks themselves are related, nor that they
share common assumptions. Rather, it means that just as a person then dwelled in his cultural framework in order to comprehend the real, so also a similar relationship obtains for a
person who today dwells in a framework in order to understand
an aspect of reality. Moreover, the distance that separates
the two frameworks allows the inquirer to identify what the assumptions of the past age were and thus enables him to distinguish between what was assumed as a means of expressing an affirmation about some aspect of reality and what was the intent
of the affirmation. Because of this foundation in the structure
of knowing, a historian can gradually come to dwell in a historical framework and understand reality through the form of
indwelling it presupposed. The isomorphic relationship between
the historical culture and his own allows him to expose faith-
fully the intended meaning and significance of a historical
document.

We must keep in mind, however, that just as today there

are various levels of indwelling corresponding to various levels of reality, so also in the examination of a historical document similar degrees of indwelling must be operative. If a person today does not partake of a particular degree of indwelling, he may not recognize its presence or discount its validity in the historical culture he is examining. Again it follows that for a theological understanding of the significance of events described in a past religious document it does not suffice simply to clarify the meaning of the text and the events it describes; the heuristic vision of faith is necessary to understand its religious significance.

If, for example, an inquiry into the meaning of the New Testament were to exclude a religious indwelling, it might come to an understanding of its meaning which accounted for the fact of the existence of Jesus, some general features of his life, his death by crucifixion, the impact he made on a few followers, and the assumptions of the cultural framework in which these followers expressed what he was and achieved. This sort of an inquiry thus might recognize that his disciples proclaimed that Jesus is the Christ and that by his death on the cross he saved men from their sins. But aside from recognizing these statements as claims, this inquiry cannot understand what they mean. Without appreciating a further dimension of meaning supplied by the indwelling of faith, the religious meaning of the events is lost. With the light of faith, however, their religious meaning can be understood, because faith "makes present to the intellect nonempirical aspects of these same events, their soteriological efficacy."[43] Because of this ability to enter into a past form of religious indwelling, a theologian can pursue the task of enlightening his understanding of his faith through an inquiry into the past articulations of its meaning.

Based on the clarifications derived from the historical phase of the inquiry, theological understanding moves into its second phase by formulating the meaning of its heuristic vision in terms of contemporary frameworks. Again the isomorphic relationship between various contemporary frameworks allows the theologian to assess them in relationship with each other and with the demand for faithfulness to the object of theological

inquiry. As a result of such a dialogical inquiry, the meaning
of traditional doctrines framed in modes of expression no longer current will be recast. This activity leads to systematic
formulations expressed in terms of prevailing though patterns
which serve as guides for a more adequate expression of the
meaning of faith.[44] Finally these reformulations will be utilized for proclaiming the meaning of faith today in order to
assist the contemporary community's understanding of the implications of its breaking out.

Any such attempt at a systematic formulation poses its
own inherent set of problems for the meaning of faith because
the most fundamental assumptions of our age are not clearly
known. The adequacy of a particular conceptual system for expressing the faith is difficult to judge. The danger of plac-
ing his primary allegiance to his system instead of to God is
a constant temptation to a theologian. In the final analysis
only the judgment of the theologian and the judgment of the
community of faith he serves are able to determine this. Like
the act of faith, which is a breaking out, so too the act of
reformulating the meaning of faith can be performed only through
a responsibility borne of the experience of ultimacy.

This schematic outline has attempted to explain how theological understanding functions as the mediating force derived
from the preaching of the faith in the past and directed to the
preaching of faith today. As such, therefore, theological understanding forms an organic whole. The concrete activity of
doing theology is accomplished through the collaborative effort of a community of scholars sustained by the same heuristic
vision, but with a focus on different levels of meaning and
with a utilization of different frames of reference. In this
way they rely on each other, assist each other, and correct
each other--all in the service of clarifying and purifying
their faith.

D. *A Concluding Appraisal*

The aim of this work has been to portray the outlines of
an approach which could indicate a direction toward a solution
of the problem of understanding the meaning and validity of
religious belief. An explication of the structure of human

knowing based on the thought of Michael Polanyi has served as
the basis for explaining how our knowledge is of reality even
though it is expressed through affirmations made in historically
conditioned frameworks. This analysis was then extended to account for the meaning of religious faith by considering it a
form of indwelling which sustains, and is sustained by, a breaking out toward the sacred. As a result of this breaking out a
heuristic vision is tacitly upheld, and by theological reflections its implications for the understanding of man and the world
are explored in the context of a specific religious tradition.

The treatment of this problem consequently has been approached and formulated within a particular perspective. Like
any framework, therefore, our study has its own limitations.
Nevertheless probing the problem at the foundational level has
distinct advantages. Because of the comprehensiveness of this
inquiry, it results in a perspective with significant and far-
reaching ramifications which may serve both by uncovering fundamental deficiencies in certain frameworks normally not noticeable and, what is more important, by contributing substan-
tively and creatively to the development of theological issues
treated by other frameworks. In fact the extent to which it
can be developed successfully by a dialogue with other theological perspectives will be one of the decisive factors for assessing the validity of this approach to the understanding of
religious belief. Unfortunately a thorough examination of such
possible developments for our study would go far beyond its
intent. Therefore, a concluding appraisal based on comparisons
with a selection of contemporary theological concerns and positions must suffice for a preliminary indication of the potential scope of our inquiry.

The most significant contribution of this foundational
inquiry undoubtedly consists in its ability to formulate the
question of religious belief. Through this formulation the
meaning of faith as a cognitional activity has been clarified
and an understanding of its transcendent object as symbolically
known has been disclosed.

Moreover, this understanding of religious belief is based
upon a general explanation of the dynamic structure of human
knowing. Consequently the foundational inquiry, in addition to

its significance for formulating the question of religious belief, provides a basis for assessing the implications of various contemporary frameworks for theological understanding.
This is achieved by means of an explication of the cognitional
activity presupposed whenever man comes to understand various
aspects of reality and their corresponding levels of meaning
through his reliance on a diversity of articulate frameworks.
Since all human intellectual endeavors are continuous from the
foundational perspective, the following appraisals can be made:
the relationship of faith to the lived experience of predominant cultural frameworks (including scientific understanding),
the relative adequacy of various philosophical approaches for
expressing the meaning of faith, and even the critical grounds
establishing a particular mode of theological understanding
(including the criteria for its own self-understanding in relationship to the larger cultural setting and to other theological positions).

With respect to modern secular culture, then, a foundational inquiry attempts to seek out and clarify the forces sustaining the culture's sense of identity and sense of reality.
Insofar as "reason," "objectivity," "facts," or "autonomy"
might make contemporary man view religious language as naive,
an assessment of currently held cultural presuppositions is a
necessary precondition for a mature faith. As a result of an
examination of the basis for these predominating notions--as
our earlier analysis of critical reason has attempted--one
should be able to come to a recognition of their ground in the
experience of ultimacy. By raising this foundational question
in the face of cultural presuppositions, the religious dimension would appear to be at least possible and perhaps even
meaningful.[45]

In contemporary Western society scientific understanding
is undoubtedly one of the most pervasive forms of experiencing
the world. Its cultural predominance is such that it is frequently taken as the norm for all understanding. Since theological thought wishes to address contemporary man, this form
of understanding must be taken into account. The danger lurking in this effort, however, is the temptation to assess religion in terms of the methods and assumptions of science.

Therefore there is a need for a foundational inquiry into the basis of scientific understanding which can clarify its methodological limitations and the aspects of reality it comprehends. When the scientific enterprise is examined in this light and its insights are incorporated into a theological frame of reference, the results can be an integrated world view wherein a theology of nature provides a basis for an understanding of man and God which is consistent with the religious tradition and need not take refuge exclusively in "personal existence" or "salvation history."[46]

In a somewhat similar vein, a foundational inquiry would necessitate a clarification of the methods and assumptions of the social-scientific study of religion. Quite frequently this discipline, perhaps because of an unreflective reliance on the methods of the physical sciences, attempts to treat the religious phenomenon as an "object." From the foundational perspective, the question of the validity of this approach should be raised: does an objective inquiry, in the commonly accepted scientific sense, distort the reality of religion? Or, does it lead, as Robert Bellah has suggested, to a "symbolic reductionism"?[47] If so, then some modifications in this approach are required which can recognize the meaning of religious symbols by partaking to some degree of its form of indwelling.

Another indication of the importance of a foundational inquiry for religious belief in terms of general cultural frameworks is its role as a guide for framing the context of moral decisions. The leaders of any social group--be they on the local or national level of political or ecclesiastical government--will make their judgments from within their cultural horizons. Normally this provides a sufficient basis for decision. At times, however, this becomes a form of imprisonment, where the leaders apply outmoded standards to new situations and new contexts unthought of previously, which results in questionable policies. Religiously, such failures have led to the rise of men with prophetic insight who, having broken beyond the limits of their cultural horizons, bear witness to a higher reality and to new norms of judgment. But there is also a need for a more balanced kind of critique, one with the broader appeal that comes from an inquiry into the presuppositions of a moral judgment and an exposition of a balanced alternative.[48] Without such an assessment of assumptions and a re-ordering of priorities through a foundational inquiry into fundamental conceptions, the properly religious values may easily be overlooked or their intent may be falsified by following the "letter" instead of the "spirit" of the norm.

On the technical philosophical level, the importance of a foundational inquiry becomes more pronounced because of the need to articulate the meaning of religious belief in terms of contemporary philosophical perspectives. Here the ability to phrase properly the question of the meaning of religious belief is crucial. The failure to do this, for example, is the primary objection to those linguistic philosophers who accept the validity of the formulation of the religious question expressed in terms of the falsification principle.[49] Unless the formulation of the question itself is assessed and seen to be wanting through a foundational analysis, the outcome of any "debate" is a foregone conclusion because of the restrictions inherent in the very framing of the question.

On the other hand, for those in the linguistic tradition, such as Ian Ramsey, who have surpassed this limitation, the positive contribution of linguistic analysis to the understanding of religious discourse can be consolidated by a foundational inquiry. Insofar as it is recognized that "no attempt to make the language of the Bible conform to a precise straightforward public language--whether that language be scientific or historical--has ever succeeded,"[50] a conclusion is reached similar to that of our own analysis. Moreover the notion of contextual disclosures revealing dimensions of reality is reminiscent of the increasingly deeper degree of indwelling required to recognize higher levels of reality. Evidently, then, a foundational inquiry would be able to help clarify the relationship between such levels of meaning. At this point a dialogue between the foundational and linguistic concerns could promote the task of clarifying the meaning of religious language, in addition to providing a mutual enrichment of the two perspectives.[51]

A thorough exposition of this function which a foundational inquiry can fulfill would require the further assessment of other modes of philosophical discourse.[52] Since we are concerned here only with outlining the main features for appraising its role in religious understanding, this would take us too far beyond the scope of our study. Hopefully this brief examination of its possible contributions to the school of language analysis suffices as an example indicating how a foundational inquiry may provide a basis which can assess the adequacy of contemporary philosphical approaches for articulating the meaning of faith.

Finally the significance of a foundational inquiry may be appraised insofar as it contributes to theological understanding itself. At this level a foundational inquiry permits an explanation of the grounds for theological understanding as such. Its primary task here is to clarify a contemporary self-understanding, including any necessary critiques, which then establishes the meaningfulness of the recourse to the symbols of the religious tradition. The great temptation here is to short-circuit this process by an immediate appeal to the past which bypasses the demands of contemporary cultural consciousness. Whenever this is done, not only are the limitations of contemporary perspectives criticized, but much of their positive significance is viewed negatively as well. Thus we could raise at this point the specific question whether Karl Barth and the magisterial tradition of neo-Thomism have not succumbed to this in their respective ways. On the other hand, it would appear that Paul Tillich recognized the importance of such foundations when, by means of the method of correlation, he attempted to explore the meaning of religious symbols precisely insofar as they were recognized to be valid expressions of problems uncovered by an existential-ontological analysis.[53]

In addition to this task of articulating the grounds for theological understanding, there is the related effort of explaining how a particular theological explication of a religious tradition judges its categories and method to be valid and adequate in terms of the demands of faith. From this vantage point a foundational inquiry can assist theological systematization by questioning its assumptions and clarifying where they need to be corrected or explored more thoroughly so that the systematic exposition may be a more faithful instrument for expressing the meaning of faith. We shall now illustrate the significance of this facet of a foundational inquiry by examining briefly the approach set forth recently by Wolfhart Pannenberg.

Pannenberg has attempted to express the meaning of Christian faith in terms of an indirect self-revelation of God mediated as universal history.[54] This endeavor raises an important question at the foundational level. In what sense can the apocalyptic tradition it investigates, precisely *as history*, mediate indirectly the revelation of God as the proleptic anticipation of the end of history?[55] Of course, Pannenberg's intention is clear. He wishes to restore a harmony between faith and reason by arguing that historical reason (as opposed to "autonomous reason") must demonstrate the basis for religious self-understanding through historical facts.[56] But this leads him, perhaps because of his reactions against the existentialist interpretation of eschatology, to place a burden on historical reason which it seemingly cannot bear. Moreover, his restriction of the meaning of faith to *fiducia*[57] does not adequately describe its character as breaking out.

The problem Pannenberg has uncovered is nevertheless valid. A foundational inquiry could assist in its resolution by exposing some of the elements of the problem in need of clarification. One suggestion is that Pannenberg's analysis must distinguish the historical and religious levels of meaning, both of which may be conveyed through the events. Then the continuity between historical and religious forms of indwelling must be explored. Based on these reflections there may emerge an explanation of the dependence of the heuristic vision of faith on historical events, which at the same time acknowledges that the distinctively religious significance of the events can be perceived only through the indwelling of faith. From the foundational perspective, an analysis of this sort is still required of Pannenberg. Perhaps such a clarification will yet be forthcoming.

Through this study we have tried to present an account of the meaning and validity of religious belief expressed in terms of the framework of Polanyi's theory of personal knowledge. In its most general features, tacit knowing combines the active role of the knower with his passive acceptance of reality perceived through given horizons to enlighten the significance of his own self-understanding. Through the dynamics of appropriation and surrender, we make ourselves. Insofar as man discovers his meaning in the universe, he is both *doer and recipient*. In religious indwelling both of these are at peak intensity, for here man receives what he himself cannot do. In this sense faith is the most profound form of doing because it derives from the most radical kind of surrender.

As a result, faith is an enduring component in the consciousness of the believer which provides an integration of the meaning of human life. This meaning is understood by dwelling in the heuristic vision of faith. In this respect religious understanding is continuous with the cognitional structure sustaining the understanding issuing from all human intelligent undertakings. The full realization of the meaning of faith, therefore, becomes open to men only insofar as their "hearing the word" transforms them. According to Polanyi's analysis, this means that men must becomes, as James exhorts, "doers of the word" (1:22).

NOTES TO CHAPTER V

1. A recent example of an analysis of this problem from a historical and typological point of view may be found in Herbert Richardson, *Toward an American Theology* (New York: Harper & Row, Publishers, 1967), pp. 30-49. See also the following classical expressions of this problem: Etienne Gilson, *Reason and Revelation in the Middle Ages* (New York: Charles Scribner's Sons, 1938), and H. Richard Niebuhr, *Christ and Culture* (New York: Harper & Row, Publishers, Torchbook Edition, 1956).

2. See Avery Dulles, *The Survival of Dogma* (Garden City, N.Y.: Doubleday & Company, Inc., 1971), p. 44.

3. Alfred North Whitehead, *Religion in the Making* (Cleveland: The World Publishing Company; Meridian Books, 1960), pp. 76-77.

4. Carl Michalson, *The Rationality of Faith*, p. 24. This work by Michalson represents one of the most thoroughgoing and lucid arguments in favor of this position. The thoughts expressed here are derived primarily from his exposition of its rationale.

5. *Ibid.*, p. 31.

6. *Ibid.*, pp. 25-26, 29.

7. Michalson, it should be pointed out, is well aware of this and seems to subscribe to the Kantian framework. See Michalson, pp. 25-26, 37, and 46.

8. *Ibid.*, p. 31.

9. *Ibid.*, p. 39.

10. This is, in fact, precisely what Michalson is forced to concede: "One ought not to say as Socrates did (*Phaedrus* 230 C) that 'landscapes teach us nothing,' but only that if and when they do so inform us about the fundamental meaning of human existence, they are not in those moments classifiable as nature but as history" (*Ibid.*, p. 29). He does not, however, clarify how any such move is made.

11. For example, see *Ibid.*, p. 30 and 42 where Michalson makes points similar to ours.

12. See *The Study of Man*, pp. 73-93 for Polanyi's detailed treatment of the relationship between science and history from the vantage point of the theory of tacit knowledge.

13. "Faith and Reason," 244.

14. *The Study of Man*, pp. 94-95.

15. "Science and Man's Place in the Universe," p. 71; see also

"Science and Religion: Separate Dimensions or Common Ground?" *Philosophy Today*, VII (Spring, 1963), 12.

16. "Faith and Reason," 246; see also "Science and Religion: Separate Dimensions or Common Ground?" 12-14.

17. "Faith and Reason," 244.

18. See above, p. 131.

19. Mircea Eliade, *The Sacred and the Profane*, translated by Willard Trask (New York: Harper & Row, Publishers; Torchbook edition, 1961), p. 28; see also pp. 12 and 210. In *Cosmos and History*, translated by Willard Trask (New York: Harper & Row, Publishers; Torchbook edition, 1959), pp. 34-35, Eliade makes a similar point by comparing the implicit ontology of primitive religious symbols to Plato's theoretical ontology.

20. For a general explanation of the notion of "breaking out" and its relationship to indwelling, see *Personal Knowledge*, pp. 195-202.

21. Joseph Maréchal, through a survey of psychological and philosophical studies on the question of the knowledge of reality and its relationship to the phenomenon of mysticism, argues for such a conclusion. See his *Studies in the Psychology of the Mystics*, translated by Algar Thorold (Albany: Magi Books, 1964), especially pp. 57-135.

22. *Personal Knowledge*, pp. 197-198.

23. *Ibid.*, p. 199.

24. See Karl Rahner, *Spirit in the World*, pp. 179-187 for an explanation of this point from the perspective of Transcendental Thomism.

25. See above, p. 164.

26. This appraisal of the limits of our conceptual systems in dealing with the sacred is adapted from Victor Preller, *Divine Science and the Science of God*, pp. 159-163 and 191-195.

27. For a more thoroughgoing explication of this thesis, see Karl Rahner, *Hearers of the Word*.

28. *Personal Knowledge*, p. 266; see also *The Tacit Dimension*, pp. 61-62.

29. *De libero arbitrio*, II, ii, 6 as quoted in Erich Przywara, *An Augustine Synthesis* (London: Sheed and Ward, 1936), pp. 58-59. For the range of Augustine's thoughts on the dynamics of faith and understanding leading to vision, see the collection of his writings arranged by Przywara on pp. 41-93.

30. See *Personal Knowledge*, p. 267.

31. Here is one way Augustine expresses this point: "We are guided in a twofold way, by authority and by reason. In time, authority has the prior place; in matter, reason . . .Thus it follows that to those desiring to learn the great and hidden good it is authority which opens the door. And whosoever enters by it and, leaving doubt behind, follows the precepts for a truly good life, and has been made receptive to teaching by them, will at length learn how pre-eminently possessed of reason those things are which he pursued before he saw their reason, and what that reason itself is, which, now that he is made steadfast and equal to his task in the cradle of authority, he now follows and comprehends, and he learns what that intelligence is in which are all things. . ." *De ordine*, II, ix, 26 as quoted in Przywara, *An Augustine Synthesis*, p. 54.

32. *The Tacit Dimension*, pp. 80-81. The context in which Polanyi is speaking is that of scientific discovery, but it is an equally appropriate description of the transition to religious indwelling.

33. For a more technical discussion of this facet of religious language, see Preller, *Divine Science and the Science of God*, pp. 241-261. See also Ian Ramsey's discussion of the categories of "disclosure" and "discernment" in *Religious Language* (New York: The Macmillan Company, 1957).

34. *Personal Knowledge*, p. 199.

35. *Ibid.*, p. 279.

36. Kenneth Schmitz, "Philosophy of Religion and the Redefinition of Philosophy," *Man and World*, III (1970), 59; the original is italicized.

37. "Pure and Applied Science and Their Appropriate Forms of Organization," 232-233.

38. *Personal Knowledge*, p. 282.

39. *Ibid.*, p. 281.

40. Thomas F. Torrance, *Theological Science* (London: Oxford University Press, 1969), p. 35. This work by Torrance is a thoroughgoing explication of the import of this principle for theological understanding.

41. *Personal Knowledge*, p. 283.

42. For a particular analysis of such a relationship between two contemporary frameworks, see Bernard Lonergan, "Isomorphism of Thomist and Scientific Thought," in *Collection*, ed. by F. E. Crowe (New York: Herder and Herder, 1967), pp. 142-151.

43. Preller, *Divine Science and the Science of God*, p. 252.

44. See *Personal Knowledge*, pp. 282-283.

45. For an outstanding example of such an inquiry, see Langdon Gilkey, *Naming the Whirlwind*.

46. For example, see Ian Barbour, *Issues in Science and Religion*. In our estimation one of the primary values of this work, in addition to its fair treatment of a wealth of material, is precisely that it carries out such a foundational inquiry into the methods and conceptions of reality presupposed by science.

47. See his "Christianity and Symbolic Realism," *Journal for the Scientific Study of Religion*, IX (1970), 89-96. It is significant that one of the positions to which Bellah appeals for his reformulation of a more integral approach is Polanyi's. Yet one should also note the responses to Bellah's address, some of them highly critical and not quite to the point, which demonstrate how ingrained certain convictions are (see pp. 97-111). For another expression of the point similar to the one we are raising here, see Wilfred Cantwell Smith, *The Meaning and End of Religion* (New York: The New American Library; Mentor edition, 1964).

48. A fine example of such an approach applied to the specific problem of abortion may be found in Daniel Callahan, *Abortion: Law, Choice and Morality* (New York: The Macmillan Company, 1970). In examining the philosophical perspectives for interpreting the data of his inquiry, Callahan is dependent on the work of Polanyi (and Grene) for articulating the difficulty in framing assumptions and, at the same time, the need for them (see pp. 351-356).

49. See Antony Flew and Alasdair MacIntyre, eds., *New Essays in Philosophical Theology* (London: SCM Press, 1955).

50. Ian Ramsey, *Religious Language*, p. 122.

51. Such a dialogue has, in fact, already begun, at least insofar as some linguistic philosophers of religion have assessed or utilized Polanyi's theory of knowledge. See Ian Ramsey, "Polanyi and J. L. Austin," in *Intellect and Hope*, ed. by Langford and Poteat, pp. 167-197. For an extensive study of religious language which discusses some of the basic epistemological aspects of Polanyi's theory of knowledge (but not their ontological implications) and develops them in light of Ramsey's reflections, see Jerry H. Gill, *The Possibility of Religious Knowledge* (Grand Rapids, Mich.: William B. Eerdmans Publishing Company, 1971).

52. That this is possible can be seen by noting briefly that Polanyi himself indicates such points of reference to Heidegger (*Personal Knowledge*, p. x) and Merleau-Ponty ("The Logic of Tacit Inference," p. 155 and "The Structure of Consciousness," pp. 221-222). Yet while Polanyi's understanding of indwelling certainly has parallels to

Heidegger's being-in-the-world, it goes beyond this insofar as it establishes the human subject in the community
and grounds his relationship to nature—both of which are
quite important for a contemporary articulation of religious belief. And although Polanyi's understanding of
the tacit reliance on our bodily processes is remarkably
like Merleau-Ponty's description of lived experience,
Polanyi's more precise articulation in epistemological
terms (including the ontological implications) would make
it more suitable, in our estimation, for expressing its
significance for religious belief. In passing we might
add that an approach which may potentially be quite fruitful from the foundational perspective is Paul Ricoeur's,
particularly insofar as he expresses the dialectic between
symbol and thought in the concluding chapter of *The Symbolism of Evil*, trans. by Emerson Buchanan (New York:
Harper & Row, Publishers, 1967), pp. 347-357.

53. See Paul Tillich, "The Problem of Theological Method,"
     Journal of Religion, XXVII (1947), 16-26.

54. See "Dogmatic Theses on the Doctrine of Revelation," in
     Revelation As History, translated by D. Granskou (New
     York: The Macmillan Company, 1968), pp. 125-158 and
     "Hermeneutic and Universal History," in *Basic Questions
     in Theology*, translated by G. H. Kehm (Philadelphia:
     Fortress Press), I, 96-136.

55. This is similar to the question raised by Moltmann when
     he asks how God can be heard in "the language of the
     facts" or how "the historic complex of particular histor-
     ic events 'itself' reveals God." See his *Theology of
     Hope*, translated by J. W. Leitch (London: SCM Press,
     1967), pp. 78 and 117.

56. See "Faith and Reason," in *Basic Questions in Theology*,
     translated by G. H. Kehm (Philadelphia: Fortress Press,
     1971), II, 46-64. About this concern Moltmann is in
     agreement with Pannenberg. See Moltmann's "The Revela-
     tion of God and the Question of Truth," in *Hope and
     Planning*, translated by M. Clarkson (New York: Harper
     & Row, Publishers, 1971), p. 25.

57. See "Insight and Faith," in *Basic Questions in Theology*,
     II, 28-45.

BIBLIOGRAPHY

This bibliography is divided into three sections which include works by Polanyi, works about Polanyi, and general works
used to develop the implications of Polanyi's thought for theology. A word about the significance of these divisions is in
order.

The first part, containing books and articles written by
Polanyi, is not intended to be complete. Because of Polanyi's
varied career and diverse interests, the scope of his published
works ranges into fields far beyond the purposes of our study.
Accordingly we have limited this bibliography to those works
which relate primarily to his analysis of human knowledge and
which contribute to the establishment of a basis for theological understanding. Moreover an attempt to compile a complete
bibliography of Polanyi's writings would be redundant. A bibliography of scientific papers authored or co-authored by Polanyi is readily available.[1] Also the thorough bibliography
of Polanyi's political, economic, social, and philosophical
writings compiled by Professor Richard L. Gelwick as an appen-
dix to his Th.D. dissertation has been brought up to date and
included in a recent publication.[2] Anyone wishing a complete
bibliography of Polanyi's writings should consult these sources.

The second part is likewise limited to works which criticize or develop Polanyi's theory of knowledge. It should be
noted that in some of the larger works contained in this section
Polanyi's thought is treated only in certain parts of the work
or it is used as a basis from which to develop further implications. The title of the work is usually a significant indication of this point. The inclusion of a particular work in
this part of the bibliography, in other words, does not necessarily imply that the entire work is devoted exclusively to an
examination of Polanyi's theory of knowledge, though this is at

times the case; rather it means that the work has some significance in understanding what Polanyi is saying.

The final part of this bibliography is a reflection of the direction in which we have moved through our expansion of Polanyi's theory of knowledge into a foundation for theology. It includes those works which have influenced the direction taken here. Some of the works are not explicitly theological, but have been included because of their relevance for clarifying the problems involved. Some have not been explicitly cited in our presentation, but their influence can be seen by the perceptive reader. Put very simply, this section provides a bibliographic overview of the context in light of which Polanyi's thought was developed.

1. *Books and Articles by Michael Polanyi*

"Beyond Nihilism." *Encounter*, XIV (March, 1960), 34-43. Also in *Knowing and Being*. Pp. 3-23.

"The Creative Imagination." *Chemical and Engineering News*, XLIV (April, 1966), 85-93.

"Do Life Processes Transcend Physics and Chemistry?" In symposium with Gerald Holton, Ernest Nagel, John R. Platt, and Barry Commoner. *Zygon*, III (1968), 442-472.

"Faith and Reason." *Journal of Religion*, XLI (1961), 237-247. Published also as "The Scientific Revolution."

"From Copernicus to Einstein." *Encounter*, V (September, 1955), 54-63.

"The Growth of Science in Society." *Minerva*, V (1967), 533-545. Also published in *Knowing and Being*. Pp. 73-86.

"History and Hope: An Analysis of Our Age." *Virginia Quarterly Review*, XXXVIII (1962), 177-195.

"The Hypothesis of Cybernetics." *The British Journal for the Philosophy of Science*, II (1952), 312-315.

"Knowing and Being." *Mind*, LXX (1961), 458-470. Published also in *Knowing and Being*. Pp. 123-137.

Knowing and Being: Essays by Michael Polanyi. Edited with an Introduction by Marjorie Grene. Chicago: University of Chicago Press, 1969.

"Life Transcending Physics and Chemistry." *Chemical and Engineering News*, XLV (August, 1967), 54-66.

"Life's Irreducible Structure." *Science*, CLX (1968), 1308-1312. Also published in *Knowing and Being*. Pp. 225-239.

"Logic and Psychology." *American Psychologist*, XXIII (1968), 27-43.

The Logic of Liberty. Chicago: University of Chicago Press, 1951.

"The Logic of Tacit Inference." *Philosophy*, XLI (1966), 1-18. Also published in *Knowing and Being*. Pp. 138-158.

"The Magic of Marxism." *Encounter*, VII (December, 1956), 5-17.

"The Message of the Hungarian Revolution." *American Scholar*, XXXV (1966), 261-76. Also published in *Knowing and Being*. Pp. 24-39.

"On Body and Mind." *New Scholasticism*, XLIII (1969), 195-204.

"On the Introduction of Science into Moral Subjects." *The Cambridge Journal*, VII (1954), 195-207.

"On the Modern Mind." *Encounter*, XXIV (May, 1965), 12-20.

Personal Knowledge: Towards a Post-Critical Philosophy. Chicago: University of Chicago Press, 1958; Harper Torchbook. New York: Harper & Row, Publishers, 1964.

"The Potential Theory of Adsorption." *Science*, CXLI (1963), 1010-1013. Also published in *Knowing and Being*. Pp. 87-96.

"Problem Solving." *The British Journal for the Philosophy of Science*, VIII (1957), 89-103.

"Pure and Applied Science and Their Appropriate Forms of Organization." *Dialectica*, X (1956), 231-242.

"The Republic of Science: Its Political and Economic Theory." *Minerva*, I (1962), 54-73. Also published in *Knowing and Being*. Pp. 49-72.

"Science and Conscience." *Religion in Life*, XXIII (1953), 47-58.

"Science and Man's Place in the Universe." *Science as a Cultural Force*. Edited by Harry Woolf. Baltimore: Johns Hopkins, 1964. Pp. 54-76.

"Science and Religion: Separate Dimensions or Common Ground?" *Philosophy Today*, VII (Spring, 1963), 4-14.

Science, Faith and Society. Chicago: University of Chicago Press, 1946; With a New Introduction. Phoenix Books. Chicago: University of Chicago Press, 1964.

"Scientific Beliefs." *Ethics*, LXI (1950), 27-37.

"Scientific Revolution." *The Student World*, LIV (1961), 287-302. Also published in *Christians in a Technological Era*. Edited by Hugh C. White. New York: Seabury Press, 1964. Pp. 25-45. Published also as "Faith and Reason."

"Sense Giving and Sense-Reading." *Philosophy*, XLII (1967), 301-321. Also published in *Knowing and Being*. Pp. 181-207. Published also in *Intellect and Hope*. Edited by Langford and Poteat. Pp. 402-431.

"The Stability of Beliefs." *The British Journal for the Philosophy of Science*, III (1952), 217-224.

"The Structure of Consciousness." *Brain*, LXXXVIII (1965), 799-810. Also published in *Knowing and Being*. Pp. 211-224.

The Study of Man. Chicago: University of Chicago Press, 1959; Phoenix Books. Chicago: University of Chicago Press, 1963.

The Tacit Dimension. Garden City, N.Y.: Doubleday & Company, Inc., 1966; Anchor Books. Garden City, N.Y.: Doubleday & Company, Inc., 1967.

"Tacit Knowing: Its Bearing on Some Problems of Philosophy." *Review of Modern Physics*, XXXIV (1962), 601-616. Also published, in an abrdiged form, in *Knowing and Being.* Pp. 159-180.

"The Two Cultures." *Encounter*, XIII (1959), 61-64. Also published in *Knowing and Being.* Pp. 40-46.

"The Unaccountable Element in Science." *Philosophy*, XXXVII (1962), 1-14. Also published in *Knowing and Being.* Pp. 105-120.

"What Is a Painting?" *American Scholar*, XXXIX (1970), 655-669.

2. *Books and Articles about Polanyi*

Adams, E. M. "The Theoretical and the Practical." *Review of Metaphysics*, XIII (1960), 642-662.

Bellah, Robert N. "Christianity and Symbolic Realism." *Journal for the Scientific Study of Religion*, IX (1970), 89-96.

Brownhill, Robert J. "Michael Polanyi and the Problem of Personal Knowledge." *Journal of Religion*, XLVIII (1968), 115-123.

Buchanan, James M. "Politics and Science: Reflections on Knight's Critique of Polanyi." *Ethics*, LXXVII (1967), 303-310.

Burt, Cyril. "Personal Knowledge, Art, and the Humanities." *Journal of Aesthetic Education*, III (April, 1969), 29-46.

Causey, Robert L. "Polanyi on Structure and Reduction." *Synthese*, XX (1969), 230-237.

Gelwick, Richard L. "Michael Polanyi: *Credere Aude*, His Theory of Knowledge and Its Implications for Christian Theology." Th.D. dissertation, Pacific School of Religion, Berkeley, 1965.

_____. "Michael Polanyi--Modern Reformer." *Religion in Life*, XXXIV (1965), 224-234.

Gill, Jerry H. *The Possibility of Religious Knowledge.* Grand Rapids, Mich.: William B. Eerdmans Publishing Company, 1971.

_____. "The Tacit Structure of Religious Knowing." *International Philosophical Quarterly*, IX (1969), 533-559.

Gilkey, Langdon. *Religion and the Scientific Future*. New York: Harper & Row, Publishers, 1970.

Grene, Marjorie, ed. *The Anatomy of Knowledge*. Amherst: University of Massachusetts Press, 1969.

Grene, Marjorie. *The Knower and the Known*. London: Faber & Faber, 1966.

Knight, Frank H. "Virtue and Knowledge: The View of Professor Polanyi." *Ethics*, LIV (1949), 271-284.

Langford, Thomas A. "Michael Polanyi and the Task of Theology." *Journal of Religion*, XLVI (1966), 45-55.

Langford, Thomas A. and Poteat, William H., eds. *Intellect and Hope: Essays in the Thought of Michael Polanyi*. Durham: Duke University Press, 1968.

The Logic of Personal Knowledge: Essays Presented to Michael Polanyi. London: Routledge & Kegan Paul, 1961.

Manser, Anthony. "A Review of *Knowing and Being*." *Philosophical Books*, XI (May, 1970), 21-23.

Michalson, Carl. *The Rationality of Faith*. New York: Charles Scribner's Sons, 1963.

Millholland, D. W. "Beyond Nihilism: A Study of the Thought of Albert Camus and Michael Polanyi." Ph.D. dissertation, Duke University, Durham, N.C., 1966.

Roberts, Paul C. "Politics and Science: A Critique of Buchanan's Assessment of Polanyi." *Ethics*, LXXXIX (1969), 235-241.

Scott, William T. "A Course in Science and Religion Following the Ideas of Michael Polanyi." *The Christian Scholar*, XLVII (Spring, 1964), 36-46.

Wagener, James W. "Toward a Heuristic Theory of Instruction: Notes on the Thought of Michael Polanyi." *Education Theory*, XX (Winter, 1970), 46-53.

3. General Works Related to Method in Theology

Barbour, Ian G. *Issues in Science and Religion*. Englewood Cliffs, N.J.: Prentice-Hall, Inc., 1966.

Burke, T. Patrick, ed. *The Word in History*. New York: Sheed and Ward, 1966.

Collins, James. *The Emergence of the Philosophy of Religion*. New Haven: Yale University Press, 1967.

Dewart, Leslie. *The Foundations of Belief*. New York: Herder and Herder, 1969.

Dulles, Avery. *The Survival of Dogma*. Garden City, N.Y.: Doubleday & Company, Inc., 1971.

Dunne, John S. *A Search for God in Time and Memory*. New York: The Macmillan Company, 1967.

Eliade, Mircea. *Cosmos and History*. Translated by Willard R. Trask. Harper Torchbook. New York: Harper & Row, Publishers, 1959.

_____. *The Sacred and the Profane*. Translated by Willard R. Trask. Harper Torchbook. New York: Harper & Row, Publishers, 1961.

Flew, Antony and MacIntyre, Alasdair, eds. *New Essays in Philosophical Theology*. London: SCM Press, Ltd., 1955.

Gilkey, Langdon. *Naming the Whirlwind: The Renewal of God-Language*. Indianapolis: The Bobbs-Merrill Company, 1969.

Gilson, Etienne. *Reason and Revelation in the Middle Ages*. New York: Charles Scribner's Sons, 1938.

High, Dallas M., ed. *New Essays on Religious Language*. New York: Oxford University Press, 1969.

Kant, Immanuel. *Critique of Pure Reason*. Translated by F. Max Mueller. Anchor Books. Garden City, N.Y.: Doubleday & Company, Inc., 1966.

_____. *Prolegomena to Any Future Metaphysics*. Translated by Lewis White Beck. Indianapolis: The Bobbs-Merrill Company, 1950.

Kaufmann, Walter. *Critique of Religion and Philosophy*. New York: Harper & Brothers, Publishers, 1958.

Kuhn, Thomas S. *The Structure of Scientific Revolutions*. Phoenix Books. Chicago: University of Chicago Press, 1964.

Lonergan, Bernard. *Collection*. Edited by Frederick Crowe. New York: Herder and Herder, 1967.

_____. "The Dehellenization of Dogma." *New Theology No. 5*. Edited by Martin E. Marty and Dean G. Peerman. New York: The Macmillan Company, 1968. Pp. 156-177.

_____. "Functional Specialties in Theology." *Gregorianum*, L (1969), 485-505.

_____. *Insight: A Study of Human Understanding*. London: Longmans, Green and Co., Ltd., 1957.

_____. *The Subject*. Milwaukee: Marquette University Press, 1968.

_____. "Theology and Man's Future." *Cross Currents*, XIX (1969), 452-461.

Maréchal, Joseph. *Studies in the Psychology of the Mystics*. Translated by Algar Thorold. Albany, N.Y.: Magi Books, Inc., 1964.

McShane, Philip, ed. *Foundations of Theology*. Notre Dame: University of Notre Dame Press, 1972.

Michalson, Carl. *Worldly Theology*. New York: Charles Scribner's Sons, 1967.

Moltmann, Juergen. *Hope and Planning*. Translated by Margaret Clarkson. New York: Harper & Row, Publishers, 1971.

_____. *Theology of Hope*. Translated by James W. Leitch. London: SCM Press, Ltd., 1967.

Muck, Otto. "The Logical Structure of Transcendental Method." *International Philosophical Quarterly*, IX (1969), 342-362.

_____. *The Transcendental Method*. Translated by William D. Seidensticker. New York: Herder and Herder, 1969.

Moran, Gabriel. *Theology of Revelation*. New York: Herder and Herder, 1966.

Newman, John Henry. *An Essay in Aid of a Grammar of Assent*. Image Book. Garden City, N.Y.: Doubleday & Co., Inc., 1955.

Niebuhr, H. Richard. *Christ and Culture*. Harper Torchbook. New York: Harper & Row, Publishers, 1956.

Novak, Michael. *Belief and Unbelief*. New York: The Macmillan Company, 1965.

_____. *The Experience of Nothingness*. New York: Harper & Row, Publishers, 1970.

Pannenberg, Wolfhart. *Basic Questions in Theology*. 2 vols. Translated by George H. Kehm. Philadelphia: Fortress Press, 1970-1.

Pannenberg, Wolfhart, ed. *Revelation As History*. Translated by David Granskou. New York: The Macmillan Company, 1968.

Preller, Victor. *Divine Science and the Science of God*. Princeton, N.J.: Princeton University Press, 1967.

Przywara, Erich. *An Augustine Synthesis*. London: Sheed & Ward, 1936.

Rahner, Karl. *Hearers of the Word*. Translated by Michael Richards. New York: Herder and Herder, 1969.

_____. *Spirit in the World*. Translated by William Dych. New York: Herder & Herder, 1968.

_____. *Theological Investigations*. 5 vols. Baltimore: Helicon Press, 1961-66.

Ramsey, Ian T. *Religious Language*. New York: The Macmillan Company, 1957.

Richardson, Herbert W. *Toward an American Theology*. New York: Harper & Row, Publishers, 1967.

Ricoeur, Paul. *The Symbolism of Evil*. Translated by Emerson Buchanan. New York: Harper & Row, Publishers, 1967.

Schmitz, Kenneth L. "Philosophy of Religion and the Redefinition of Philosophy." *Man and World*, III (1970), 54-82.

Smith, Wilfred Cantwell. *The Meaning and End of Religion*. Mentor Books. New York: New American Library, 1964.

Teilhard de Chardin, Pierre. *The Phenomenon of Man*. Translated by Bernard Wall. New York: Harper & Brothers, 1959.

Tillich, Paul. "The Problem of Theological Method." *Journal of Religion*, XXVII (1947), 16-26.

Torrance, Thomas F. *Theological Science*. London: Oxford University Press, 1969.

Tracy, David. *The Achievement of Bernard Lonergan*. New York: Herder and Herder, 1970.

Whitehead, Alfred North. *Modes of Thought*. New York: Capricorn Books, 1958.

_____. *Religion in the Making*. Meridian Book. Cleveland: The World Publishing Company, 1960.

Wittgenstein, Ludwig. *Philosophical Investigations*. Translated by G. E. M. Anscombe. New York: The Macmillan Company, 1953.

202

NOTES TO BIBLIOGRAPHY

1. This bibliography has been compiled by John Polanyi in
    The Logic of Personal Knowledge, pp. 239-247.

2. See *Intellect and Hope*, edited by Langford and Poteat, pp.
    432-446. Gelwick also includes here a thorough list of
    reviews on Polanyi's works.